D0380091

BEST OF

Dubai

Terry Carter & Lara Dunston

Colour-Coding & Maps

Each chapter has a colour code along the banner at the top of the page which is also used for text and symbols on maps (eg all venues reviewed in the Highlights chapter are orange on the maps). The fold-out maps inside the front and back covers are numbered from one to five. All sights and venues in the text have map references; eg, (5, A2) means Map 5, grid reference A2. See p96 for map symbols.

Prices

Multiple prices listed with reviews (eg Dh10/5) usually indicate adult/concession admission to a venue. Concession prices can include senior, student, member or coupon discounts. Meal-cost and room-rate categories are listed at the start of the Eating and Sleeping chapters, respectively.

Text Symbols

- ☎ telephone
- ✉ address
- 🖳 email/website address
- 💲 admission/rates
- 🕓 opening hours
- ⓘ information
- ♿ wheelchair access
- ✖ on-site/nearby eatery
- 🚼 child-friendly venue
- Ⓥ good vegetarian selection

Best of Dubai
1st edition – Feburary 2006

Published by Lonely Planet Publications Pty Ltd
ABN 36 005 607 983

Australia Head Office, Locked Bag 1, Footscray, Vic 3011
  ☎ 03 8379 8000 fax 03 8379 8111
  🖳 talk2us@lonelyplanet.com.au
USA 150 Linden St, Oakland, CA 94607
  ☎ 510 893 8555 toll free 800 275 8555
  fax 510 893 8572
  🖳 info@lonelyplanet.com
UK 72–82 Rosebery Avenue, London EC1R 4RW
  ☎ 020 7841 9000 fax 020 7841 9001
  🖳 go@lonelyplanet.co.uk

This title was commissioned in Lonely Planet's Melbourne office and produced by: **Commissioning Editor** Kerryn Burgess **Coordinating Editor** Lucy Monie **Coordinating Cartographer** Anthony Phelan **Layout Designer** Jacqueline McLeod **Editor** Kate Evans **Managing Editor** Suzannah Shwer **Cartographer** Hunor Csutoros **Managing Cartographer** Shahara Ahmed **Project Manager** Chris Love **Mapping Development** Paul Piaia **Desktop Publishing Support** Mark Germanchis **Thanks to** Eoin Dunlevy, Quentin Frayne, Victoria Harrison, Sally Darmody, Adriana Mammarella

Photographs by Lonely Planet Images and Phil Weymouth except for the following: p77 Michael Coyn; p28 Greg Elms; p7, p10, p41, p68, p69, Izzet Keribar; p5, 26, p30, p35, p37, p65, p74, p79, p80 Chris Mellor; p42 Guy Moberly; p18, p33, p34, p43, Christine Osborne; p6, p39, p67, Neil Setchfield; p29, 38 Wayne Walton; p8, p27, p31 Tony Wheeler. **Cover photograph** Skyline with flowers in foreground, Sheikh Zayed Rd, Phil Weymouth/Lonely Planet Images.

All images are copyright of the photographers unless otherwise indicated. Many of the images in this guide are available for licensing from Lonely Planet Images: www.lonelyplanetimages.com.

ISBN 1740596196

Printed through The Bookmaker International Ltd.
Printed in China

Contents

From the Publisher

THE AUTHORS
Terry Carter

Terry has lived in Dubai since 2003 and the United Arab Emirates (UAE) since 1998, after many years working in Sydney's publishing industry. Having erroneously concluded that travel writing was a far more glamorous occupation than designing books or websites, he's been travel writing for several years and has travelled extensively throughout the Middle East during his time in the UAE. Terry has a master's degree in media studies and divides his time between freelance travel writing, photography and web design, while based in incessantly sunny Dubai, where he ironically spends most of his time indoors.

Lara Dunston

Despite a lifelong passion for travel – Lara has been to 50 countries at last count – moving to the UAE certainly didn't seem a logical choice for someone with a Russian-Australian heritage and a master's degree in Latin American cinema and Spanish! But the opportunity to develop the creative talent of young Emirati women and contribute to the growth of a film culture was too hard to refuse. Seven years later, Lara acknowledges that her students have taught her as much about Dubai and Emirati culture, tradition and shopping (!) as she's taught them about film and media.

LONELY PLANET AUTHORS

Why is our travel information the best in the world? It's simple: our authors are independent, dedicated travellers. They don't research using just the Internet or phone, and they don't take freebies in exchange for positive coverage. They travel widely, to all the popular spots and off the beaten track. They personally visit thousands of hotels, restaurants, cafés, bars, galleries, palaces, museums and more – and they take pride in getting all the details right, and telling it how it is. For more, see the authors section on **www.lonelyplanet.com**.

PHOTOGRAPHER
Phil Weymouth

Australian-born Phil Weymouth and his family called Tehran, Iran, home from the late 1960s until the revolution in 1979. After studying photography in Melbourne, Phil returned to the Middle East in the mid-1980s to live and work as a photographer in Bahrain. Now based again in Melbourne, Phil visited Dubai for this assignment, and marvelled at how staggeringly fast the city changes. Between snapping images, Phil enjoyed the warm hospitality of the people, watching the *abras* (water taxis) jockey for position on the Creek, and washing down lamb *shwarma* (meat and tomatoes in pita) with hot sweet tea.

Introducing Dubai

Dubai is a surreal combination of Vegas without the gambling, Disneyland sans the mouse and '60s Beirut with megabucks to burn, where visitors are treated like millionaires and oblige by acting like them. A city on fast-forward, where every new venture is bigger, brighter, more eccentric and expensive than the last – an orgiastic wave of development that shows no signs of crashing on its five-star hotel–lined shores. So what is it that this city has to offer that keeps tourist numbers heading skyward as fast as Dubai skyscraper construction? Sunshine is guaranteed, and there's stunning shopping, non-stop nightlife, fantastic hotels and world-class events in a city with touches of the exotic old Middle East, without touts and terrifying taxi rides.

Dubai has a history of tempting people to visit; ever since Sheikh Maktoum bin Hasher al-Maktoum, ruler of a fledgling Dubai, lured foreign traders away from other Middle East destinations by offering a safe, tax-free port in 1894, Dubai has welcomed guests with open arms. More than a century later, Dubai's entrepreneurial descendents are attracting more than five million visitors a year and in typically ambitious form expect this to increase to 15 million by 2010.

These numbers leave other popular Middle East tourist destinations shaking their collective heads and – whisper it – feeling a little jealous. There's no doubt that Dubai lacks the ancient features and cultural legacies that cities such as Marrakech or Cairo can offer, but then Dubai is unlike any other Middle East destination – a real life rags to riches story without an end in sight.

An intriguing juxtaposition of the old and the new: the Dhow Wharfage (p15) and city skyline

Neighbourhoods

Dubai has four main areas of interest to visitors: **Deira**, **Bur Dubai**, **Sheikh Zayed Rd** and **Jumeirah**. With most of the development of the city spreading in parallel down Sheikh Zayed Rd and Jumeirah, some residents call this 'the new centre of Dubai', while Deira and Bur Dubai represent 'old' Dubai.

Deira, which is located on the north side of the Dubai Creek is home to most of the atmospheric souqs, as well as some wonderful historic buildings and the fascinating Dhow Wharves. There are several good hotels on the Creek and in the surrounding area, plenty in the direction of the airport, but not much else of interest to visitors in this direction – except for the obligatory visit to City Centre Mall. Bur Dubai is on the south side of Dubai Creek and includes the historic **Bastakia** area and the fascinating Dubai Museum. Bur Dubai is also home to a multicultural mix of residents in **Karama** and **Satwa**, while the rest of Bur Dubai is an eclectic mix of hotel-residences, apartment blocks and an escalating number of streetwalkers.

Sheikh Zayed Rd is host to Dubai's exhibition centre as well as having a number of outstanding business hotels, many of which contain first-rate restaurants and clubs. Running parallel to Sheikh Zayed Rd, Jumeirah Rd (also known as Beach Rd) is the home of the Jumeirah area. This fashionable sprawl is where Dubai's luxurious beach resorts are located, as well as some interesting boutiques that are hidden in the myriad malls that span the length of Jumeirah Rd. The overwhelming emphasis in this area is on restaurants, bars and beaches – so if relaxing and ray-catching are the goals of your visit, this is the place to stay. This beach resort strip is so popular that Dubai's leaders decided to perform several encores in the shape of offshore islands that will more than double the amount of coastline.

OFF THE BEATEN TRACK
- Sure it's hard to get a booking at **Al Maha Resort** (p69, below), but this very private resort offers unrivalled peace and tranquillity.
- A morning at **Creekside Park** (p22) is a blissful escape right in the centre of the city.
- Take an early-morning beach dip before Dubai wakes up at any of Dubai's beach **Parks** (p22) or open beaches with a sea-level view of the Burj Al Arab (p10).
- Take a late afternoon stroll through **Karama** (2, A4) or **Satwa** (3, E2) and you'll barely spot a Birkenstock-shod tourist.

Itineraries

Heritage House (p20): a completely restored traditional house on the Deira side of Dubai Creek

Traditional Dubai

Start with the **Heritage and History Walking Tour** (p31), in **Bastakia** (p9) and end at the **Heritage Village** (p13). After a traditional lunch at **Kanzaman** (p62), take an *abra* (water taxi) to Deira, checking out **Al-Ahmadiya School** and **Heritage House** (p20) for more Dubai history. Your evening **Desert Safari** (p18) offers a slice of Bedouin life, with camel riding, henna, *sheesha* (water pipes) and belly dancers.

Luxury Dubai

Rejuvenate with a jet-lag treatment at **Six Senses Spa** (p27) and continue spoiling yourself with shopping at **Souq Madinat Jumeirah** (p39). Refuel at fabulous **Zheng He's** (p57) before taking the hotel limo to Dubai's **BurJuman Centre** (p38) for exclusive **Saks Fifth Avenue** (p41) and **Tiffany & Co** (p42). Hit the souqs for gold and perfume and then refresh before cocktails at **Burj Al Arab** (p68), dinner at **Eauzone** (p55), while your VIP table awaits you at **Trilogy nightclub** (p62).

Sports-Mad Dubai

The cooler months offer Dubai's major sporting events and plenty of outdoor action. Have a round of golf at the **Emirates Golf Club** (p26), assuming that the **Dubai Desert Classic** (p59) isn't on! Watching the **Dubai Tennis Championships** (p59)? Sip an ale outdoors at the **Irish Village** (p60). Here for the **Rugby 7s** (p59)? Check out a local **football game** (p66), or watch the horses go round at the **Dubai International Racing Carnival** (p65).

DUBAI LOWLIGHTS

- the ceaseless traffic…
- being stuck in said traffic when it's a 45°C summer's day
- live music – if it's not a Filipino cover band, it's UB40 on tour
- waiters so inept they'd forget their name if it wasn't pinned on their chest

Highlights

DUBAI MUSEUM (2, C2)

This engaging museum is a must for visitors, not only for its whimsical dioramas but also because it vividly charts the rapid progress of Dubai. A couple of hours spent at the museum before exploring the rest of Dubai really helps put the speedy evolution of the city into perspective.

INFORMATION

- ☎ 353 1862
- 🖳 www.dubaitourism.ae
- ✉ Al-Fahidi St, Bur Dubai
- 💲 adult/child Dh3/1
- ⏱ 8.30am-8.30pm Sat-Thu, 2.30-8.30pm Fri
- ℹ brochure
- ♿ fair
- ✗ Basta Art Café (p51)

The museum is housed in the Al-Fahidi Fort, built c 1787 to defend Dubai Creek. After serving as both the residence of Dubai's rulers and the seat of government, it became a museum in 1971. After entering the museum courtyard, you'll see several small boats and a *barasti* (palm-leaf) house, with traditional wind-tower 'air conditioning'. The hall on the right houses displays featuring *khanjars* (curved daggers) and other traditional weapons; the hall to the left of the courtyard has a video of traditional Emirati dances, a display of musical instruments and more weapons.

The real treat, however, awaits you in the large display halls that are underground. After a multimedia presentation of the development of the city, there is a series of dioramas representing the past commercial life of Dubai as well as domestic life, desert life and life on the sea. The vivid scenes – complete with disconcertingly lifelike dummies – are augmented with hologram-like video projections and an atmospheric soundtrack. Photography isn't allowed, but the desire of most visitors to be photographed next to one of the historical characters keeps the museum guards very busy!

After these vivid tableaux, the archaeological displays are bound to disappoint all but the most dedicated fan of digs. Everyone else will head straight for the decent gift shop.

DON'T MISS

- trying out the effect of the wind-tower air-con
- checking out the impressive front door – procured from the house of Sheikh Saeed al-Maktoum
- trying to sneak a photograph with one of the historical characters, sans flash

BASTAKIA QUARTER (2, C2)

This small, densely concentrated neighbourhood of narrow lanes and wind-towered residences was once home to wealthy Persian traders, mainly from Bastak in southern Iran, lending the neighbourhood its name, Bastakia. These merchants, dealing mostly in pearls and textiles, settled in Dubai because of its tax-free trading and accessible creek.

Most of the houses here date back to the early 1900s and the prosperous merchants constructed their homes from coral and lime-stone, a step up from the more modest building materials offered by the ubiquitous palm tree. This is one of the main reasons that the buildings in Bastakia have lasted – they were far more durable and more valuable than the traditional *barasti* hut made from palm fronds.

INFORMATION
🚹 fair; construction work in the area
🍴 Bastakiah Nights (p51)

DON'T MISS
• the only remaining foundations of the city wall
• the original carved wooden doors and brass door knockers that remain on some of the houses
• hearing the call to prayer from the nearby mosques echo through the streets

While there is some debate as to the origin of the wind-tower concept, there's no doubting that towers and courtyards were common features of Iranian coastal buildings. The towers take the hot air upwards and out of the building and also pick up breezes and direct them downwards.

The Bastakia has now mostly been restored and the quarter is starting to develop a lovely arty feel. Courtyard buildings you can visit include XVA (p73), a wonderfully restored house that is a hotel, gallery and café, and the traditionally decorated Bastakiah Nights restaurant (p51). As you wander through the narrow, peaceful lanes you can easily imagine the life of the merchant residents at the turn of the 20th century.

A window to the past: Bastakia Quarter

BURJ AL ARAB (4, D1)

It would be difficult to find a more fitting a symbol of Dubai today than the audacious and iconic Burj Al Arab (Arabian Tower). The world's tallest dedicated hotel, the sail-shaped building tops out at an impressive 321m and was the boldest and most ambitious of the myriad 1990s projects undertaken by Crown Prince Sheikh Mohammed. The ambitious Sheikh knew that a world-class city – which he was determined to make Dubai – needed an iconic symbol like the Eiffel Tower.

INFORMATION

- ☎ 301 7777
- 🖳 www.burj-al-arab.com
- ✉ Jumeirah Rd, Umm Suqeim
- 💲 booking of restaurant (with credit card) required, min Dh175 per person
- ♿ excellent
- ✗ Majlis Al Bahar (p55)

The process of construction began on the world's only 'seven star' (actually rated five-star luxury) hotel in 1994, with pillars of the offshore island plunging 40m into the seabed. It wasn't until 1999 that the hotel opened its doors to its first awestruck guests who marvelled at the white woven glass-fibre screen sail façade and then were bewildered by the 'Arabian fantasy' interior.

It's as though the imagination that fuelled the design of the extraordinary exterior of the hotel had run out of puff after filling the *dhow* (traditional wooden boat) sail, leaving the building's beauty decidedly skin deep. The interior seeks to impress with its sheer extravagance, having left taste exhausted at the door and, while everything that glitters here *is* gold, colours that match gold are only randomly in evidence. Perplexingly, the interior designer has stated that there was no specific colour scheme – perhaps another world first for Dubai right there! As for the rooms, suffice it to say you half expect an Arabian Joan Collins to make an entrance via the internal staircase.

The cost of construction of the hotel has never been made public, but it clearly was money well spent as Sheikh Mohammed could then happily tick off 'iconic symbol' on his formidable to-do list for Dubai.

DON'T MISS

- watching the exterior lights change hue at night
- admiring the Burj from Bahri Bar (p59)
- visiting the Skyview (p61) cocktail bar, to be found a dizzying 200m above the Gulf

DEIRA GOLD SOUQ (2, C1)

Dubai owes its well-deserved reputation as the City of Gold to the Deira Gold Souq – its sheer scale impresses even veterans of Middle East gold markets. Considered to be the largest gold bazaar in Arabia, it attracts buyers from across the region.

In many Gulf countries and the Subcontinent, a good dowry is one that's heavy with gold. The bride is laden with ornate jewellery on her wedding day, and, as gold given to a bride must be new, tradition alone keeps a fairly constant flow of customers coming to Dubai.

Every conceivable kind of jewellery is available – earrings, rings (for fingers, nose and toes), necklaces, chains, pendants, bracelets, bangles, anklets, headdresses and amulets. Designs range from traditional to modern, cutting-edge to conservative. If you can't find it, you can always commission it! Artisans can create whatever style you want and can alter the composition of alloys to create pink, white, yellow or green hues of gold.

Make sure to visit the souq in the evening when the glittering gold and shimmering gems are at their most jaw-dropping and the restored wooden-latticed lanes are at their most atmospheric.

INFORMATION

- ✉ on & around Sikkat al-Khail St, btwn Deira Souq & Old Baladiya Sts
- ☺ 10am-10pm Sat-Thu, 4-10pm Fri
- ♿ fair
- ✖ Ashwaq Cafeteria (p57)

The families of veiled Gulf women bargain for pieces for their daughters' dowries, while 'Jumeirah Janes' (see the boxed text, p28) guide their visiting guests, armed with long shopping lists. It's particularly worth noting that many shops close between 1pm and 4pm, especially during summer, so this is not the best time of day to visit.

At the eastern end of the gold souq is a small perfume souq, where a staggering range of Arabian and European fragrances are sold, from the latest designer brands to heady Arabian *attars* (perfumes), worth buying for the kitsch packaging alone.

DON'T MISS

- the elaborate and intricately detailed gold bridal headdresses and necklaces, often only worn on wedding days!
- the garish window-display mannequins dressed as Oriental princesses
- taking home a little gold something…

DEIRA SPICE SOUQ (2, C2)

The air of the atmospheric old alleys of the Spice Souq on the Deira waterfront is heady with the aromas of spices, herbs, nuts, pulses, dried fruits and chillies. Sacks overflow with frankincense and *oud* (fragrant wood), ground cardamom, cumin, paprika and saffron, cinnamon sticks and cloves, as well as the local favourites, which are sumach and *zaatar* (thyme). Inside the shops, shelves are lined with orange- and rosewater; henna powders; incense burners and charcoal; and various other products, both ancient and modern, from pumice stones and traditional wooden tooth cleaners, to hair colours and cake mixes.

INFORMATION
- ✉ Al-Sabkha Rd, Deira
- 🕐 10am-1pm & 4-10pm Sat-Thu, 4-10pm Fri
- ♿ limited
- ✖ Ashwaq Cafeteria (p57)

The souq's wooden archways and wind towers are restored, but the market, established in the 1830s, would have an antique quality if it weren't for the odd shop selling plastic kitchenware and toys. Focus instead on the spice sellers, taking time to stop and smell the bouquet of aromas.

By far the most popular buy, with local ladies and tourists alike, is frankincense. The best quality crystals come from the harvested gum resin of trees in the Dhofar area of Oman. Frankincense can be bought by weight although these days spice sellers prepackage the crystals in kits that include a small clay or decorative incense burner and coal. Ask for a demonstration on how to prepare the incense. Emiratis burn incense on a daily basis, often passing it around after meals, and at weddings and parties, so that the smoke perfumes guest's clothes. Tiny boxes of saffron, rose-water and henna are also great buys and make exotic souvenirs.

DON'T MISS
- asking what's what in those spice sacks!
- buying a bag of frankincense, some magic coal and an incense burner
- looking up at the restored wind towers

Let your nose guide the way at the Spice Souq

WATERFRONT HERITAGE AREA (2, B1 & C1)

This evocative heritage area offers up a wonderful building-design and photography exhibition in Sheikh Saeed al-Maktoum House as well as the fascinating step back in time that you'll find in the Heritage and Diving Villages. Both make an excellent late-afternoon jaunt, especially when they are combined with a visit to the Bastakia Quarter (p9), followed by a relaxing meal and *sheesha* (water pipe).

The house of Sheikh Saeed al-Maktoum, who was the grandfather of Dubai's present ruler, is a listed national monument that has been beautifully restored as a museum to record and show the development of Dubai. The 30-room house was built in 1896 during the reign of Sheikh Maktoum bin Hasher al-Maktoum and was the family residence with Sheikh Saeed living here until his death in 1958. The house was reopened as a museum in 1986, and by far the most absorbing of its exhibits is a collection of photos of Dubai that were taken during the period from 1948 to 1953. The Marine Wing, which has photographs of fishing, pearling and boat building, is also worthy of note.

A little further towards the entrance of Dubai Creek are the Heritage and Diving Villages. In the cooler months and also during Ramadan these attractions are filled with locals and visitors taking in the exhibits and shows. The Heritage Village re-creates traditional Bedouin and village life, complete with a collection of *barasti* homes, a traditional coffeehouse and a small souq that sells

INFORMATION

- ☎ Sheikh Saeed's house 393 7139, Heritage Village 393 7151, Diving Village 393 9390
- 🖳 www.dubaitourism.ae
- ✉ Al-Shindagha Rd, Bur Dubai
- 🕑 Sheikh Saeed's house 8am-8.30pm Sat-Thu, 3-9.30pm Fri; Heritage & Diving Villages 8am-10pm Sat-Thu, 8-11am & 3-10pm Fri
- ⓘ brochure
- ♿ fair; uneven paving
- 🍴 Kanzaman (p62)

Bedouin jewellery and pottery. From October to April, there are performances of local music and dance, and you can visit a practitioner of traditional medicine. The Diving Village has displays on pearl diving – before the introduction of the cultured pearl, this was key to the livelihood of the city – and boat building.

DON'T MISS

- the wonderful detail of the restoration of Sheikh Saeed's house
- seeing if you're game to try traditional *Al Hijama* (cupping) medical therapy
- the young girls doing the 'hair dance' at the Heritage Village

BUR DUBAI SOUQ (2, C2)

Established in the 1830s, Dubai's souqs have long had a reputation as the best in Arabia, and with good reason. Like the Deira Gold and Spice Souqs, Bur Dubai Souq is a bustling bazaar with great bargaining opportunities, interesting architecture and lots of atmosphere.

INFORMATION

✉ btwn Bur Dubai waterfront & Al-Fahidi St, Bur Dubai
🕙 10am-1pm & 4-10pm Sat-Thu, 4-10pm Fri
♿ limited
🍴 Basta Art Café (p51)

In reality the 'souq' encapsulates several shopping areas. The covered souq by the waterside, with its restored wind towers, houses small shops with Russian signage in their windows selling vibrant textiles, Arabian 'antiques' and collectables, sequinned slippers and curly-toed Aladdin shoes from Afghanistan and Pakistan; this souq also proffers tacky souvenirs, cheap T-shirts and clothes, and Indian sweet shops. Along with the alley between the Sikh Gurudaba and Hindu Shri Nathje Jayate temples (p25), which has shops selling religious paraphernalia, bindis, garlands of flowers and incense, this area is the most atmospheric.

Less aesthetically pleasing, yet still intriguing, are the surrounding lanes and streets, which contain more textile and sari shops, haberdashers and tailors. Al-Fahidi St, also considered to be part of the souq, is lined with shops selling jewellery, shoes, stationery, souvenirs, electronics – and luggage to take it all home!

The souq is best explored at night when it's crowded and lively, and in winter for cool breezes. Take time in between bargaining to talk

DON'T MISS
• picking up a pair of Aladdin slippers
• attempting to translate the Russian signage in the shop windows
• trying the Indian sweets from the small stands

to the salesmen. They hail from everywhere, from Mumbai to Islamabad, Isfahan to Kiev. The shoppers are just as varied, from tourists haggling over suitcases to local ladies looking for the latest textiles.

As much a daily event as dinner, in Dubai shopping is taken as seriously as eating

DUBAI CREEK & DHOW WHARFAGE (2)

A walk along Dubai Creek and the Dhow Wharfage on a cool evening is a wonderful Dubai experience. Small fishing villages were settled on the Creek as long as 4000 years ago, and modern creek life traces its birth back to the 1830s when the Maktoum branch of the Bani Yas tribe settled in the area and established a free trade port, luring merchants from Persia. The houses built on the banks can bee seen on the History and Heritage Walking Tour (p31).

The Dhow Wharfage still very important to small Gulf traders and offers visitors a fascinating insight to the difficult lives of the sailors. The wharfage extends all the way from the port customs offices next to Maktoum Bridge to the Spice Souq, and *dhows* bound for every port from Kuwait to Iran, and from India to Oman, dock here loading and unloading their cargo day and night. You'll see stacks of goods waiting to be transferred, including tyres, mattresses, plastic chairs air-conditioning units, washing machines, small cars – even some kitchen sinks!

Creekside Park is a more peaceful vantage point to Dubai Creek, while hiring an *abra* (water taxi) gets you closer to the hustle and bustle. Further along the Creek, on the far side of Al-Garhoud Bridge, at the *dhow*-building yard (5, E2) you can see the *dhows* being constructed and repaired by hand, using traditional tools and teak woods. However, not everything at the yard is done as it has been for centuries: sometimes the local boys pop an engine in after it's finished!

INFORMATION
✉ Baniyas Rd, Deira; Creekside Park, Bur Dubai
♿ limited
✖ Glasshouse Mediterranean Brasserie (p49)

DON'T MISS
• saying *salaam* (greetings) to the sailors to score an invitation on board
• playing 'spot the most unusual type of cargo'
• the toilets on the back of the dhows – yes, they really are toilets!

Dubai Creek and the Dhow Wharfage: where tradition meets technology

JUMEIRAH MOSQUE (3, D1)

The Jumeirah Mosque is an attractive sight among the cookie-cutter villas and malls of the north end of Jumeirah Rd. Its modern Islamic architecture has splendidly subtle details in the stonework, especially visible in the two minarets. Non-Muslims are generally not allowed to enter mosques, but you can make a visit under the auspices of the Sheikh Mohammed Centre for Cultural Understanding, set up by Dubai's Crown Prince. These organised tours are run twice a week and are aimed at fostering better understanding between Muslims and other religions and cultures – something clearly needed in this time of misinformation and stereotyping.

INFORMATION

- ☎ 353 6666
- 🖥 www.culture.ae
- ✉ Jumeirah Rd, Jumeirah
- 🕙 10am Thu & Sun (tour)
- ♿ fair
- 🍽 Lime Tree Café (p55)

The exteriors of mosques are generally far more attractive and intricately detailed than the interiors (large open areas are required inside for worship), but the tour affords you a chance to not only get a peek at the mosque, but to ask questions about the mosque and the Islamic faith. In this question-and-answer session you can find out more about the call to prayer, the haj (pilgrimage to Mecca) or the five pillars of Islam.

DON'T MISS

- the detail of the minarets
- having some questions about Islam ready
- checking out the mosque at night, when it's superbly lit

Visitors are expected to dress modestly (no shorts) and women are required to wear a headscarf; visitors must also remove their shoes before entering the mosque.

Make a pilgrimage to Jumeirah Mosque

MADINAT JUMEIRAH (4, C1)

The magnificent Madinat Jumeirah (Jumeirah City) might be a holiday resort, but it has become a home away from home for many local and expat residents, who repeatedly return here for shopping, eating, drinking, and dancing. Don't miss the chance to check it out.

Take in the fabulous Arabian-inspired architecture and the rich interiors of the splendid luxury hotels, Al-Qasr (p69) and Mina A' Salam (p68) before venturing into the meandering lanes of the mazelike Souq Madinat Jumeirah (p39). Admire the interior architecture while you shop!

There are numerous entertainment choices within the resort – choose from a musical at the Madinat Theatre (p64), jazz at JamBase (p63), an *oud* player in the central plaza, or DJ at Trilogy (p62) – and the eating options are endless. There are waterside cafés such as Dôme (p52), casual eateries such as the Noodle House (p53), atmospheric water-view restaurants such as Shoo Fee Ma Fee (p57), and buzzy bars like LeftBank (p60).

INFORMATION

☎ 366 8888
🖥 www.madinatjumeirah.com
✉ Al-Sufouh Rd, Jumeirah
🕐 10am-10pm
♿ good
✗ Shoo Fee Ma Fee (p57)

However, what everyone loves best about this Oriental fantasy palace is the water – there's water everywhere, and plenty of vantage points are provided from which to view it. If you see a flight of stairs, take it, it'll most probably lead to a lovely rooftop space with a sublime water view. Meander around the restaurant promenades for a closer look, and, if you're staying at one of the hotels or have a hotel restaurant booking, you can take a fun *abra* ride along the Venice-like canals to get there. In the evening, settle in on the terrace at the Agency (p59) for absolutely mesmerising views – you won't want to leave!

DON'T MISS

• admiring the architectural details
• taking the time to browse in the many shops
• sitting at a restaurant or café by the waterside…and sighing deeply

DESERT SAFARI

You could be forgiven for thinking that Dubai is nothing more than five-star hotels and shopping malls, but Emiratis themselves never lose their affinity with the desert. A half-hour drive quickly replaces the long shadows cast by Dubai's skyscrapers with the sensuous shadows created by desert dunes.

INFORMATION

- ☎ Arabian Adventures 343 9966, Net Tours & Travels 266 8661
- 🖥 Arabian Adventures www.arabian -adventures.com, Net Tours & Travels www.nettoursdubai.com
- ✉ Arabian Adventures Emirates Holidays Bldg, Interchange No 2, Sheikh Zayed Rd, Net Tours & Travels Al-Bakhit Centre, Abu Baker al-Siddiq Rd, Hor al-Anz
- 💲 from Dh260
- 🕐 safaris usually leave midafternoon and return 9-10pm
- ♿ fair, requires separate vehicle; some difficulties due to soft sand
- ✗ provided

The desert safaris offered by the companies that are listed in the box (left) can be tailored to suit your wishes, but the standard safari on offer usually departs in the afternoon from Dubai (you'll be picked up at your hotel) and from there travels into the desert. Your driver soon transforms the 4WD into an amusement-park ride with a little 'dune-bashing' in an approved area of the desert, before you reach the camp.

When you arrive there's enough time for activities such as a camel ride or some sand boarding before witnessing a beautiful desert sunset and, after working up an appetite, enjoying a Middle East barbecue feast. After dinner you will have a chance to try some *sheesha*, attempt to match the hip-twisting moves of a belly dancer or get some henna tattoos before heading back into Dubai.

If you haven't experienced the desert before and don't plan on paying a visit to one of the desert resorts (see the boxed texts, p69 and p70), a desert safari day trip is a fuss-free way of getting a taste of (a glamorised version of) Bedouin life. If you're a time-poor traveller it's also a great way to tick off some of those 'must-do' Dubai activities. If you really crave that Bedouin experience, you can also stay overnight in the camp – the stars that fill the desert sky late at night are a real treat. Two recommended providers are Arabian Adventures (5, D2) and Net Tours & Travels (2, E5).

DON'T MISS

- the sunset photo opportunity, preferably with silhouetted camels
- being hypnotised by the belly dancer's hips
- trying *sheesha* at least once

SHEIKH ZAYED ROAD (3)

While everyone speeds down this eight-lane highway in a hurry to get to Media City or Abu Dhabi, it's worth taking a turn-off and heading for a hotel with a view to check out the architecture on this strip. Several hotels have opened up here in the last couple of years and Sheikh Zayed Rd appears to be host for some freeform architectural jazz, where each new development riffs off the last. The tuning fork–shaped Dusit Dubai hotel (p69) and the four-pronged Fairmont (p70) with its evening light show are two fine specimens. A bird's-eye view of these can be had from Vu's Bar (p61).

The road is also beginning to be referred to as 'the Strip', in line with its transformation into a glamorous shopping 'strip' and Las Vegas–type pleasure 'strip' – without the gambling! Of all the ritzy hotel shopping arcades and small exclusive malls, Emirates Towers' Hotel's Shopping Blvd is the best – home to the Sheikh of Chic's Villa Moda (p41), Jimmy Choo (p40), Gucci, Armani and other top designers. Some of Dubai's best restaurants, bars, clubs and cafés are on the strip between the World Trade Centre and Interchange 1 – Marrakech and Hoi An, the Agency and Lotus One, Tangerine and Zinc – all of which are tucked away in five-star hotels. The strip is also home to numerous *sheesha* cafés – full of beautiful, young, smartly dressed Arabs, smoking *sheesha,* drinking coffee, and watching other beautiful young people.

INFORMATION
- ✉ Sheikh Zayed Rd
- 🕐 10am-late, some shops closed 1-4pm
- ♿ shopping centres offer good access
- 🍴 Marrakech (p53)

DON'T MISS
- • admiring the amazing hotel architecture and interiors – everywhere!
- • the ritzy shopping at Emirates Towers: Jimmy Choo (p40), Azza Fahmy (p42), Villa Moda (p41)
- • smoking *sheesha* with the beautiful people at Cosmo Café (p62)

The only way is up: Emirates Towers (p70) on Sheikh Zayed Rd

HERITAGE HOUSE & AL-AHMADIYA SCHOOL (2, C1)

The Dubai Museum (p8) offers visitors selected vignettes of past Dubai life, whereas the Heritage House is a completely restored traditional house on the Deira side of Dubai Creek. Built in 1890, it was first home to a wealthy Iranian merchant, and then in 1910 the residence to Sheikh Ahmed bin Dalmouk, a key player in Dubai's pearling industry. It was restored in 1994.

INFORMATION

☎ 226 0286
🖳 www.dubaitourism.ae
✉ Al-Ahmadiya St, nr Gold Souq, Deira
🕙 Sat-Thu 8am-7.30pm, Fri 2-7.30pm
ⓘ brochures available
♿ fair; ground fl only
🍴 Ashwaq Cafeteria (p57)

The *majlis* (meeting room) is the first room in the house and typically this is where guests are welcomed. Privacy – especially for the women of the house – is valued and there is a separate women's *majlis* to the left of the spacious courtyard. The courtyard itself is a common feature of Gulf houses as it provides light and cooling air to the surrounding rooms, all of which have been restored to represent their original function.

Situated directly behind Heritage House is the Al-Ahmadiya School – no coincidence as Sheikh Ahmed commissioned and funded the school. It's the oldest school in Dubai with the first phase of construction completed in 1912. Schools in this era of Dubai were semiformal and were funded by wealthy merchants such as Sheikh Ahmed, as formal education was not established in Dubai until 1956. Teaching in these schools was based around learning the Quran, but various other subjects were taught as well.

The school is fully restored and combined with a visit to the Heritage House offers a wonderful slice of Dubai life from the early 20th century.

DON'T MISS
• the Heritage House's bride's room
• noting the cooler temperature of the Heritage House's courtyard
• photos in the Al-Ahmadiya School of Sheikh Mohammed as a child and the 'activities' for boys such as jumping through flaming hoops!

A display of traditional education at Al-Ahmadiya School

Sights & Activities

MUSEUMS & GALLERIES

Art Space (3, E3)

A refreshingly focused contemporary gallery dedicated to promoting national and international work, developing appreciation for art, and nurturing the local scene. Art Space has shown pop art by Emirati Mohamed Kanoo and powerful work by Iranian women artists. New exhibitions each month with glam opening nights. ☎ 332 5523 🖳 www.artspace-dubai.com ✉ Fairmont, Sheikh Zayed Rd 🕒 10am-8.30pm Sat-Thu

Green Art Gallery (3, C2)

Concentrating on the work of UAE artists, regardless of nationality but particularly those influenced by the Arab world, its people, heritage, culture and environment, the gallery is committed to developing talent by educating artists about international art distribution and promotion. Exhibitions change regularly. ☎ 344 9888 🖳 www.gagallery.com ✉ behind

Local art is a feature at Majlis Gallery (below)

Dubai Zoo, Jumeirah 🕒 9.30am-1.30pm, 4.30-8.30pm, closed Fri

Majlis Gallery (2, C2)

The city's oldest gallery, established in the 1970s, is situated in a charming courtyard house in the historic Bastakia neighbourhood. Primarily exhibiting paintings, Islamic calligraphy and sculpture by local artists, there are also high-quality locally produced pottery, ceramics, glassware and handicrafts. ☎ 353 6233 ✉ Al-Fahidi Roundabout, Bur Dubai

🕒 9.30am-1.30pm & 4-7.30pm Sat-Thu

Majlis Ghorfat Um-al-Sheef (4, F1)

This gypsum and coral rock two-storey *majlis* (meeting place) was built in 1955 and was attended in the evenings by former ruler Sheikh Rashid bin Saeed al-Maktoum where he would listen to his people's complaints, grievances and ideas. Beautifully preserved and wonderfully decorated, it offers an authentic snapshot of Dubai during the 1950s. ✉ 17 St, off Jumeirah Rd, Jumeirah 💲 Dh2 🕒 8.30am-1.30pm & 3.30-8.30pm Sat-Thu, 3.30-8.30pm Fri

Third Line (4, D2)

Talented young Dubai curators Sunny Rahbar and Claudia Cellini have opened one of the more adventurous art spaces in Dubai. Exhibitions have included challenging contemporary work that breaks the rules of traditional arts, such as Pakistani miniatures or Persian calligraphy, to create refreshing new forms. ☎ 394 3194 🖳 www.thethirdline.com ✉ next to the

---

ART STARTER

The idea that Abu Dhabi is the intellectual capital of the UAE, Sharjah the cultural heart and Dubai the centre of business is changing with an art scene starting to flourish in Dubai. Sharjah's successful seventh international art biennial put the UAE on the arts map and gave local artists exhibition opportunities. While Dubai's older galleries like Green Art are committed to nurturing local talent by educating artists, fresh young things like Art Space and the Third Line are run by young curators committed to giving contemporary artists a voice and teaching the Dubai public a thing or two about art. Just as importantly, they're injecting glamour into the art scene with splashy champagne openings!

PUBLIC ART

Dubai is hooked on public art, as you'll soon see driving along the city's streets — colourful painted camels and horses seem to dominate every intersection and roundabout. First there was the *Camel Caravan* and more recently *The Celebration of the Arabian Horse*. The beasts are bought bare of decoration by corporate sponsors or donated by sheikhs to individuals, schools, colleges and universities, and professional, amateur and student artists paint their beloved creatures before they're auctioned off by Christies at a glamorous gala event with proceeds to charities. Over US$1 million has been raised with local sheikhs easily outbidding multinational CEOs. There are already whispers about the next public art project…might giant falcons grace the city's greens?

Courtyard, off Sheikh Zayed Rd, Interchange 3, Al-Quoz ☺ 11am-8pm Sat-Thu, 4-8pm Fri

Total Arts at the Courtyard (4, D2)

Situated in a courtyard complex with artists' workshops, designers, craftspeople and media companies, Total Arts holds changing exhibitions of modern and traditional art, Islamic calligraphy, Persian miniatures, rare carpets, textiles and sculptures by local and regional artists. ☎ 228 2888 ⌨ www .courtyard-uae.com ✉ the Courtyard, off Sheikh Zayed Rd, Interchange 3, Al-Quoz ☺ 10am-1pm & 4-8pm Sat-Thu

XVA (2, C2)

This beautifully restored Bastakia residence houses an art gallery with temporary exhibitions, a café and a quiet boutique hotel (p73) with rooms on the upper floor. ☎ 353 5383; ⌨ xva@ xvagallery.com ✉ behind

Basta Art Café, Al-Musallah Roundabout, Bur Dubai ☺ 9.30am-8pm Sat-Thu

PARKS, BEACHES, GARDENS & ZOOS

Al-Mamzar Park (5, F1)

This attractive park covers a small headland on the northern outskirts of Dubai, with scenic views of Sharjah, opposite. The small beaches in the park have lifeguards and there are changing facilities, barbecues and kiosks as well as a swimming pool and children's play areas. There are also chalets for rent; note that Wednesday is for women and children only. ☎ 296 6201 ✉ Al-Mamzar Park, Deira $ person/car Dh5/30 ☺ 8am-10.30pm

Creekside Park (5, E2)

This oasis of green stretches from Al-Garhoud Bridge towards Al-Maktoum Bridge and makes for a delightful escape from the heat and humidity of Dubai's streets. It has children's play areas — as well as the outstanding Children's City (p28) – *dhow* (traditional wooden boat) cruises, kiosks, restaurants, a cable car, an amphitheatre and beaches (though swimming in the Creek is not recommended). ✉ Dubai Creek, Bur Dubai $ Dh5 ☺ 8am-11pm

A Dubai favourite: Jumeirah Beach Park (opposite)

Sat-Wed; 8am-11.30pm Thu, Fri & public holidays; women & children only Wed

Dubai Wildlife & Waterbird Sanctuary
(5, D2)

Dubai's pink flamingo population flocks to the inland end of the Creek during the winter months. Also known as Al-Khor Nature Reserve, new viewing platforms at this sanctuary allow visitors to get a close-up view of the birds without disturbing them and the juxtaposition of these elegant birds with the Dubai metropolis is dramatic.

☎ 206 4240 ⌷ Oud Metha Rd, Ras al-Khor ⏱ 10am-6pm Sat-Thu

Dubai Zoo (3, C1)

While plans to relocate this former private zoo to a more spacious address appear to have stalled, local anger at the cramped conditions has grown. Just the sight of the tiny giraffe enclosure from Jumeirah Rd should be enough to deter you. If the kids want to see exotic animals, it's safer to turn on the Discovery Channel at the hotel.

☎ 349 6444 ⌷ Jumeirah Rd, Jumeirah ⑂ Dh3 ⏱ 10am-5pm Wed-Mon

Jumeirah Beach Park
(4, F1)

With its palm trees, grass, shady areas and long stretch of beach, this is Dubai's favourite park; it's especially crowded at weekends. Facilities are excellent, with a children's play area, barbecues, picnic tables, walkways and kiosks as well as lifeguards on duty.

☎ 349 2555 ⌷ Jumeirah Rd, Jumeirah ⑂ person/car Dh5/20 ⏱ 8am-10.30pm, women & children only Sat

Safa Park (4, F2)

Popular with residential families, the facilities on offer are enough to keep everyone happy. There is a lake with paddleboats, tennis courts, a soccer pitch, barbecues and an artificial waterfall.

☎ 349 2111 ⌷ cnr Al-Wasl Rd & Al-Hadiqa St, Safa ⑂ admission Dh5 ⏱ 8am-11pm, women & children only Tue

Zabeel Park (3, F3)

It was more construction zone than technology zone at the time of research, but this new technology-themed park, covering 51 hectares over three areas, is to include a lake, a jog-

ging track, various sports facilities and a club house, in addition to an Imax theatre, retail, food and beverages facilities, a 45m-high Panoramic Tower and a Technology Zone.

☎ 800 900 (Dubai Municipality) ⌷ Sheikh Khalifa bin Zayed Rd & Al-Qataiyat Rd

NOTABLE BUILDINGS

For Dubai's most notable building of all, the Burj Al Arab, see p10.

Dubai Chamber of Commerce & Industry (2, D4)

Next door to the National Bank of Dubai, this triangular building is blanketed in sheets of blue glass. From some angles the building takes on a flat appearance, like a great featureless monolith.

⌷ Baniyas Rd, Deira

Dubai Creek Golf & Yacht Club (5, E2)

When you cross the bridges over the Creek, you will notice the pointed white roof of the clubhouse set amid artificial, undulating hillocks. The idea behind this 1993

SCALING THE HEIGHTS: BURJ DUBAI

Dubai's endless attempts to be noticed on the world stage almost inevitably resulted in what will be the world's tallest building. It's predicted Burj Dubai will top out at over 705m, around 200m higher than the current title holder, Taipei 101 in Taiwan (509m).

Chicago-based architect Adrian Smith's design is elegant, inspired by the Hymenocallis flower and Islamic geometric shapes. The central core of the building will be surrounded by three elements staggered in height, creating a spiral effect when you view the building.

The all-concrete tower is expected to be finished by 2008, after which we hope the project managers – and the 20,000-odd construction workers – get a nice long holiday. For more, see www.burjdubai.com.

National Bank of Dubai (right)

UK design by Brian Johnson (for Godwin, Austen and Johnson Architects) was to incorporate a traditional element into the design – the white sails of a traditional Arab *dhow*.

☒ opposite Al-Garhoud Rd, Deira

Emirates Towers (3, D3)
Still the most outstanding architectural feat of Sheikh Zayed Rd, this pair of towers is a cloud-busting wonder of concrete and glass. The taller of the two towers is the business tower – taller than the Burj Al Arab (p10) at 355m, and the shorter tower is the hotel. Taking a glass lift from the hotel's foyer reveals that the view from the building is just as breathtaking.

☒ Sheikh Zayed Rd

Jumeirah Beach Hotel (4, D1)
Constructed to represent a breaking wave, this mammoth structure works playfully off the sail shape of the offshore Burj Al Arab (p10). Inside, the vast lobby features a vertigo-inducing mural stretching the full height of the building, with Dubai at the base and the sun at the very top.

☒ Jumeirah Rd, Umm Suqeim, Jumeirah

National Bank of Dubai (2, D4)
This shimmering bank headquarters overlooking the Creek has become one of Dubai's landmark buildings. Designed by Uruguayan-born architect Carlos Ott and completed in 1997, its curved reflective façade reflects the sun beautifully in the afternoon, creating glittering light across the Creek.

☒ Baniyas Rd, Deira

MOSQUES & TEMPLES

See p16 for the Jumeirah Mosque.

Ali bin Abi Taleb Mosque (2, C2)
Located at the rear of the fabric souq, it's notable for its sensuous bulbous domes and gently tapering minaret. While its outline is best appreciated from Baniyas Rd in Deira, on the opposite side of the Creek, the detail of the exterior is quite beautiful.

☒ Ali bin Abi Taleb St, Deira

Grand Mosque (2, C2)
Just north of the Dubai Museum, this mosque boasts the city's tallest minaret. While the mosque might appear to be a beautiful example of restoration work, it was in fact built in the 1990s in the style of the original Grand Mosque, which dated from 1900.

☒ 11c St, north of the Dubai Museum, Bur Dubai

SKIING SHEIKH ZAYED ROAD

Developments in Dubai have reached such a startling level of surrealism that the only way forward is to 'think different' – really different. Picture the planning meeting: we're building another shopping mall/entertainment complex/hotel. We need the polar opposite of what people are expecting. Polar. Ice. Snow. Ski resort!

By the time you read this, the Mall of the Emirates (Sheikh Zayed Rd, Interchange 4) will not only house one of the world's largest indoor ski slopes, including a quad chair lift and black runs, but will also offer chalets overlooking the slopes as part of a Kempinski hotel (www.kempinski.com). The resort wants visitors to absorb the full alpine experience, but you should be nervous if they ask you to wear an avalanche transceiver – they *are* striving for full immersion! For more, see www.skidxb.com.

Iranian Mosque (3, D2)
The brilliant blue mosaic tile work (below), typical of Iranian mosques and buildings, is beautifully realised in both the stunning Iranian Mosque and the Iranian Hospital, opposite.
✉ Al-Wasl Rd, Satwa

Shri Nathje Jayate Temple & Sikh Gurudaba (2, C2)
You'll recognise this temple, also known as Krishna Mandir (mandir is 'temple' in Hindi) by the lines of barefooted souls and racks of shoes outside. In the lane between here and Sikh Gurudaba tiny shops sell religious paraphernalia – flower garlands, psychedelic images of gods, spiritual cassette tapes, incense and bindis.
✉ behind the Grand Mosque & near the Creek waterfront, Bur Dubai

OUTDOOR ACTIVITIES

Dubai Creek Golf & Yacht Club (5, E2)
Situated right on the Creek, this golf course has been redeveloped with a new front nine, redesigned by Thomas Björn. There is also a new nine-hole par 3 course, a floodlit driving range, as well as a couple of restaurants taking advantage of the creekside location. Men must have proof of a handicap under 28, and for women an under-36 handicap is necessary.
☎ 295 6000 ⌨ www .dubaigolf.com ✉ near the Deira side of Al-Garhoud Bridge $ 18 holes weekdays Dh295, weekends Dh325

Dubai Desert Extreme (5, E2)
This small skate park is located in Wonderland park (p30). There's enough here to entertain most street-skate enthusiasts for a couple of hours and you can rent equipment (including the compulsory helmet) on site.
☎ 324 3222 ✉ off Al-Garhoud Bridge, Al-Garhoud

MOSQUE ARCHITECTURE

Mosques are essentially simple structures made up of a few basic elements. The most visible of these is the minaret, the tower from which the call to prayer is broadcast.

Mosques always have a mihrab, a niche in the wall facing Mecca, indicating the direction believers must face while praying. The minbar, a pulpit chair traditionally reached by three steps, dates from the Prophet Mohammed's lifetime.

The Jumeirah Mosque (p16) is based on the Anatolian style of mosque, as is the multi-domed Grand Mosque (opposite). This style is identifiable by a massive central dome. Others in Dubai are based on Iranian and Central Asian models, with more domes covering different areas of the mosque. Shiite mosques are notable for their exquisite green-and-blue faïence tile work. One stunning Dubai example is the Iranian Mosque (above).

The *dhow*-sail roof of Dubai Creek Golf & Yacht Club (p23)

WATER SPORTS

Dubai is a fantastic place for water sports, but don't forget that waterproof sunscreen! You can swim and surf on the open beaches, but stick to the patrolled beaches of the clubs if you're not a regular beachgoer as there are rips and currents.

Al-Boom Diving (3, D2)
This long-established diving centre has experienced, PADI-certified staff and offers both novice and refresher courses as well as open-water diving off Dubai and dive trips to both coasts where the water is clearer and the sea-life

$ per hr Dh10, plus park entry ☺ Sat-Wed 5-11pm, Thu & Fri 4pm-midnight

Emirates Golf Club (4, A2)
This is home to Dubai's premier golf tournament, the Dubai Desert Classic. There are two courses here of championship standard as long as you are a serious golfer – men must have proof of a handicap under 28, for women the handicap should be under 36. It's an attractive club, with the clubhouses designed to resemble Bedouin tents and excellent food on offer as well.
☎ 347 3222 ☐ www .dubaigolf.com ✉ Interchange No 5, Sheikh Zayed

Rd $ 18-hole Majlis course Dh525, 18-hole Wadi course Dh375 (Thu-Sat Dh425), plus compulsory cart rental Dh50

Montgomerie (4, A2)
This Colin Montgomerie–designed 18-hole course is set in 90 hectares of unique landscaping including huge greens – the 13th being the largest green in the world. There are also extensive practice facilities including a swing studio to get that hook or slice under control.
☎ 390 5600 ☐ www .themontgomerie.com ✉ Emirates Hills Residential Estate $ 18 holes Thu-Sat Dh595, Sun-Wed Dh475

SARTORIAL SENSITIVITY

With more than a hundred nationalities living in Dubai, it's easy to lose sight of the fact that this is a Muslim country. A disappointing trend has seen uninformed visitors and many expats (who should know better) going out dressed in clothes Emiratis find offensive – anyone who tells you that you can 'wear anything' in Dubai hasn't spoken to many Emiratis about the subject. While Emiratis are welcoming hosts and know the value of the tourist dollar, this doesn't mean it's considered acceptable to flaunt your flesh. Beachwear is fine at a beach resort, but not at a shopping mall. Your little Paris Hilton–esque number is OK for the clubs, but take a taxi there and back. Boys in shorts? If you must, but the locals think it's funny that you're walking around in your underwear!

GO FLY A KITE

Kite surfing has become very popular in Dubai and any afternoon (apart from Fridays and public holidays) at what has become known as Kite Beach (4, E1) you'll see kite surfers silhouetted against the sun as they get in a few jumps after work. Kite surfing can be a dangerous sport – especially when there are others enjoying the same stretch of beach – so the Dubai Kite Club (www.dubaikiteclub.com) was formed in 2002. In the interests of safety, all kite surfers need a licence and Wollongong Beach is the only beach where kite surfing is permitted in Dubai; however, visitors to Dubai can get a temporary licence. For more information, visit the Kite Club website.

and reefs make for excellent diving.

☎ 342 2993 🖳 www .alboommarine.com ✉ Al-Wasl Rd, Jumeirah, just south of the Iranian Mosque

Dubai Creek Golf & Yacht Club (5, E2)

You can charter a 10m boat from four to eight hours in the pursuit of some big game off Dubai. The boat takes up to six passengers and prices include the skipper, fuel, fishing tackle and bait.

☎ 205 4646 🖳 www .dubaigolf.com ✉ near the Deira side of Al-Garhoud Bridge 💲 4/8hr Dh1875/2850

Wakeboard School (5, E2)

With wonderful water temperature and normally flat water conditions, Dubai is a super place to try some wakeboarding. With an excellent boat (important to get a decent wake happening) and experienced coaches, you'll soon know your tail grab from your indie grab.

☎ 324 3308 🖳 www .thewakeboardschool.com ✉ Bur Dubai on the Creek at Jaddaf 🕐 8am-6pm 💲 about 15 mins Dh75, plus admission Dh20

PAMPERING

Cleopatra's Spa (5, E2)

Dubai's first day spa is still widely considered by locals to be its best. There's a bewildering array of packages, most being half-day treatments including lunch. Men aren't left out of the picture either – while your better half is getting the luxurious Cleopatra treatment, you can take an 'Anthony's Anti Stress' package that will help soothe the impact of the bill.

☎ 324 7700 🖳 www.cleo patras-spa.com ✉ Wafi City, Al-Qataiyat Rd, Bur Dubai

Givenchy Spa (4, A1)

There are simply gorgeous surroundings for Givenchy's signature treatments such as body scrubs and wraps as well as facials and massages – including the increasingly popular 'four hands' treatment. Men are also welcome to book for afternoon treatments.

☎ 399 9999 🖳 www .oneandonlyresorts.com ✉ One&Only Royal Mirage, Al-Sufouh Rd, Jumeirah

Six Senses Spa (4, C1)

Just being at Madinat Jumeirah is quite relaxing

Walk like an Egyptian into Cleopatra's Spa (above)

enough, but the Asian and European treatments that are on offer here will have you reaching a plateau of serenity. There is an array of fascinating alternative treatments on offer, such as crystal therapy, but the Sunburn Soother and Jet Lag Recovery are tailor-made for Dubai.

☎ 366 8888 ☐ www .madinatjumeirah.com ✉ Madinat Jumeirah, Al-Sufouh Rd, Jumeirah

Taj Spa (2, E4)

It's fitting that the speciality of this Indian hotel's spa is in Ayurvedic treatments. Ayurveda, the ancient Indian system of healing, treats individuals based on their needs, which translates to a tailored set of massage techniques, herbs and applications. This might sound a little too spiritual, but it's incredibly relaxing.

☎ 223 2222 ☐ www .tajhotels.com ✉ Taj Hotel, 23D St, Rigga

PERMA-TANNED PRINCESSES

With a hard-working husband, a maid to take care of the little ones and a gardener to keep the Jumeirah villa grounds green, the wives of Western executives on secondment to Dubai often find themselves with plenty of time on their hands. While many women find a niche and start up a business or do charity work, others take advantage of the weather, cafés and spas to transform themselves into what have become known as 'Jumeirah Janes'. Easily recognisable by their perfect nails, deep tans and trainer-toned bodies, you'll spot them in their huge SUVs on their way to the Lime Tree Café (p55) to compare notes: the best schools and new aerobic workouts are freely discussed, while the horror of one day having to go back to gloomy weather and doing your own washing are studiously avoided.

DUBAI FOR CHILDREN

Dubai is frankly one of the most child-friendly destinations in the world. Most hotels have baby-sitting services on offer, the better hotels have well-organised children's programmes and there are plenty of activities either aimed at or interesting to kids that will keep them happy for days. Meals are no problem – most restaurants have kids menus – and if they have a craving for fast food, Dubai's more than happy to oblige. Look for the kid-friendly tag (👶) in the Eating, Sleeping and Entertainment chapters for the best options to keep the little ones occupied and entertained.

Al-Nasr LeisureLand
(2, A6)

It's bigger than the Hyatt Regency (p70) rink – big enough for ice hockey – and there's also a bowling alley and fast food available.

☎ 337 1234 ✉ off Oud Metha Rd, Oud Metha 💲 including boot hire Dh10 🕐 2hr sessions start 10am, 1pm, 4pm & 7.30pm

Children's City (5, E2)

This colourful building, resembling children's building blocks, is home to a themed activities centre and children's museum, and is one place that kids absolutely love. Part of the Creekside Park (p22), activities are targeted to children's

EXPAT KIDS

Dubai is the ideal place to develop in your kids a sense of the cosmopolitan. International schools teach children Arabic and other languages. Local stores sell books like 'Islam – A-Z', and boardgames such as 'The Quran Challenge Game'! Many expats enrol their kids in another national school – our Egyptian friends send theirs to German school, while our Lebanese neighbours' kids speak English at day school, go to French school at night and speak Arabic with their family. They watch hundreds of satellite TV channels from around the world. They go to Global Village (see the boxed text, p45) each year. 'Foreign' food becomes familiar. The world becomes smaller. And we all live happily ever after.

All but the most inexpensive hotels have baby-sitting services and these are the best option for visitors. Expats with families generally have maids who watch the kids, or they borrow a neighbour's maid for the evening if they don't.

age groups and are themed, creative, educational and hands-on.

☎ 334 0808 ✉ Creekside Park, Bur Dubai $ adult/child Dh15/10 ⏱ 9am-10pm Sat-Thu, 4pm-10pm Fri

Encounter Zone (5, E2)
Wafi City's efforts to keep the little ones occupied while parents indulge in a retail therapy session is divided into two zones; LunarLand for the preteens and Galactica for everyone else. If you need baby-sitting you can use their 'Drop n' Shop' service (Dh25 per hour).

☎ 324 7747 ⌨ www.waficity.com $ under 9s per hr Dh20, over 9s per hr Dh30, all-day pass Dh45 ⏱ 10am-11pm Sat-Thu, 1-11pm Fri

Magic Planet (2, D6)
Deira City Centre (p38) is home to the cacophony created by this indoor playground for children. There's everything from a gentle carousel to those parent-bothering shoot 'em-up video games as well as a train snaking its way around the planet. A great place for

kids to work off that sugar rush after the almost obligatory fast food binge at the food court next door.

☎ 295 4333 ✉ Deira City Centre, Al-Garhoud Rd, Deira $ entry free, rides from Dh5 ⏱ 10am-midnight

Wild Wadi Waterpark (4, D1)
This waterpark does an excellent job of catering for everyone with its ingeniously interconnected rides. There

are water safety lessons for the little ones, sedate rides for young children and nervous adults, and two Flowriders (artificial waves) and the truly terrifying Jumeirah Sceirah for the more adventurous. Many people settle in for hours, with food and beverages available via a clever debit card attached to your wrist.

☎ 348 4444 ⌨ www.wildwadi.com ✉ Jumeirah Rd, Jumeirah $ adult/child (over 13) Dh140/120

Wild Wadi Waterpark (above)

Never say neigh at Godolphin Gallery (below)

🕓 11am-6pm Nov-Feb, 11am-7pm Mar-May & Sep-Oct, 11am-9pm June-Aug

Wonderland (5, E2)

This amusement park has a little of everything: a waterpark, theme park, the usual rides (for children and adults), and fast-food outlets. Hours can vary so phone ahead.
☎ 324 3222 🖳 www .wonderlanduae.com ✉ next to Al-Garhoud Bridge, opposite Grand Hyatt Hotel 💲 per ride Dh5-10 🕓 11am-10pm, waterpark 11am-8pm, theme park 4-10pm

QUIRKY DUBAI

Dubai Country Club (5, D3)

There's a reason the green fees are much cheaper at this golf club than the other clubs –

there're no greens, only browns! To use the all-sand course, players are given a patch of artificial grass to place under their ball on the fairways and the sand on the putting 'greens' is brushed smooth to approximate the rolling effect of grass.
☎ 333 1155 ✉ Ras al-Khor Rd 💲 per round Dh65

Godolphin Gallery (5, D3)

This excellent museum packed with photographs, trophies, horse-racing paraphernalia and interactive displays charts the extraordinary success of the Godolphin stables. Visited as part of a tour of Nad al-Sheba racetrack, it's a must for racing fans (see p36).
☎ 336 3666 book in advance 🖳 www.nad alshebaclub.com

✉ Nad al-Sheba, off Sheikh Zayed Rd, Interchange 2, Al-Marqadh 💲 tour & breakfast adult/child Dh130/60 🕓 7-11am Mon, Wed & Sat Sep-Jun

Ibn Battuta Mall (5, A2)

You'll feel like 14th-century Arab traveller Ibn Battuta after exploring this enormous mall. The six different 'courts' (minimalls in themselves) are in the architectural styles of the places Battuta visited, China, India, Persia, Egypt, Tunisia and Andalusia. The effect is beautiful – albeit bizarre – and only the sight of a Starbucks under the magnificent Persian dome breaks the magic.
☎ 345 6687 ✉ Sheikh Zayed Rd btwn Interchanges 5 & 6 🕓 9am-10pm Sat-Thu, 2-10pm Fri

MALL OR THEME PARK?

The opening of the themed Ibn Battuta Mall (above) is just the start of the somewhat loopy projects that take shopping to (literally) another world in Dubai. You can take the kids 'over to China' at Ibn Battuta, while the Mall of the Emirates will have you shopping for washing powder then hitting the powder snow at the indoor snowpark (p24). Alongside Mall of Arabia (the largest in the world, due for completion in 2008) will be Space and Science World, where you can don a space suit and relive the first landing on the moon. Once you figure out the moon isn't really made of cheese, you can head to the mall and pick some up...

Trips & Tours

WALKING TOURS
Heritage & History in Bur Dubai

Nothing evokes Dubai's past more than the wind towers of the **Waterfront Heritage Area** (p13) and **Bastakia Quarter** (p9). Start in **Bastakia** and explore its atmospheric lanes and restored buildings such as **Bastakiah Nights** (**1**; p51) restaurant, **XVA** (**2**; p73) gallery and hotel, **Majlis Gallery** (**3**; p21) and **Basta Art Café** (**4**; p51). Then head along Al-Fahidi St to the excellent **Dubai Museum** (**5**; p8).

Walk across to the **Grand Mosque** (**6**; p24) and past Hindu **Shri Nathje Jayate Temple** (**7**; p25) to the lane of shops selling religious paraphernalia. Continue past **Sikh Gurudaba** (**8**) to the lane's end and turn right: you're at **Bur Dubai Souq** (**9**; p14).

Walk to the waterfront and admire the wind-tower architecture. Backtrack and explore the souq, exiting at the end near **Bur Dubai abra station** (**10**). Continue along the waterfront, passing **Bin Suroor Mosque** (**11**) and recently refurbished **Sheikh Juma al-Maktoum House** (**12**). Visit **Sheikh Saeed al-Maktoum House** (**13**; p13); **Sheikh Obaid bin Thani House** (**14**), an Islamic Centre, built in 1916; the **Heritage Village** (**15**; p13); and the **Diving Village** (**16**; p13). Have lunch at **Kanzaman** (**17**; p62).

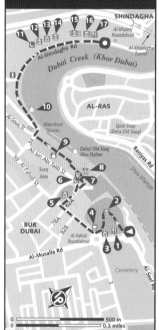

distance 3km duration 4hr (including Museum visit) ► start Al-Seef Rd Waterfront ● end Kanzaman restaurant

Sheikh Saeed al-Maktoum House (p13): air conditioning c 1896

Deira Souqs

One of Dubai's key attractions is shopping its vibrant souqs, best visited at night. Start around sunset at **Deira Old Souq abra station** (**1**). Your nose will guide you across Baniyas Rd to the atmospheric **Deira Spice Souq** (**2**; p12). When you're done, exit on Al-Abra St, turning right, then left on to Al-Ras St – these streets house wholesalers trading goods plied by the *dhows*. Turn right on Al-Hadd St and right again into Al-Ahmadiya St. Visit the beautifully restored **Heritage House** (**3**; p20) and adjacent **Al-Ahmadiya School** (**4**).

A waft of Dubai at the perfume souq (p11)

Continue along Al-Ahmadiya St, turning right into Old Baladiya St, reaching the wooden entrance to the **Gold Souq** (**5**; p11). Gold rich, but cash poor, exit the other end on to Sikkat al-Khail St and continue to the **Perfume Souq** (**6**; p11), with shops selling perfumes and incense, traditional *kandouras* and belly-dancing outfits. Make a stop at **Ashwaq Cafeteria** (**7**; p57) to refuel.

Kandouras are worn under *abeyyas*

On Al-Soor St (which becomes 67 St), take the first left into the **Deira Covered Souq** (**8**; p38) for anything from *sheesha* pipes to textiles. Exit on Al-Sabkha Rd, then cross the road and follow Naif South St to **Naif Souq** (**9**) to bargain for fake designer *abeyyas* with the local ladies!

distance 3km **duration** 3hr (excluding souq bargaining!) ▶ **start** Deira Old Souq abra station ● **end** Naif Souq

Arts & Culture in Sharjah

Dubai's neighbouring city, Sharjah, has a flourishing arts scene in its extensively renovated heritage and arts precincts. Start in the late afternoon (except Mondays when most sights are shut), visiting the former home of Sharjah's ruling family, **Al-Hisn Fort** (**1**). Cross Al-Borj Ave towards Al-Borj Rd to

The cool interior of Sharjah Heritage Museum

Al-Gharb and the Heritage Area's lovely pedestrianised space. Here, several noteworthy buildings fall under the umbrella of **Sharjah Heritage Museum** (**2**): **Bait Al-Naboodah**, which displays jewellery, costumes and artefacts; the restored **Al-Midfaa House**; and old **Souq Al-Arsah** (**3**). Refuel at its traditional coffeehouse. Next door Majlis Ibrahim Mohammed al-Midfa

has the only round wind tower in the Gulf. Nearby are the **Sharjah Islamic Museum** and **Museum for Arabic Calligraphy & Ornamentation** (**4**). Back on Al-Borj Ave, past Al-isn Fort is the Al-Shuwaihyen area. Visit **Sharjah Art Museum** (**5**), home to a good permanent collection and Sharjah's Biennial (p59). Across the square you can visit the **Sharjah Art Centre** (**6**) in Bait Al-Serkal and **Sharjah Art Galleries** (**7**) in Obaid Al-Shamsi house, with artists' studios; the **Very Special Arts Centre** (**8**) for disabled artists; the **Emirates Fine Arts Society** (**9**); and **Arts Café** (**10**).

When you're tired of art and culture, head for the Sharjah Souq

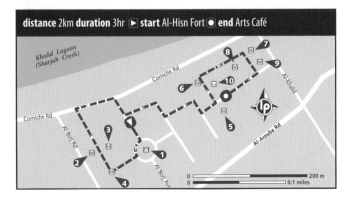

distance 2km **duration** 3hr ▶ **start** Al-Hisn Fort ● **end** Arts Café

DAY TRIPS

East Coast (1, C4)

A trip to the Indian Ocean–facing East Coast offers up some brilliant contrasts to the flat concrete jungle of Dubai. The scenic drive on the way there takes you to some fine beaches, and past rocky headlands and fishing villages. The desert landscape of the road that leads towards Al-Dhaid is punctuated with many small farms and you'll see the odd wayward camel silhouetted on a dune or crossing the road. About 20km after Al-Dhaid you'll reach the **Friday Market** (it's open every day), where the kitsch carpets are a highlight – we love the ones with the Lolita-esque faces. The northernmost town of the UAE's East Coast, **Dibba**, has a beautiful bay and little fishing villages that are worth exploring. Heading south, Al-Aqqa is home to the excellent **Le Meridien Al-Aqah Beach Resort** (☎ 09-244 9000; www.alaqah.lemeridien .com), which is perfect for an overnight stay. Visible from here is **Snoopy Island**, known for its vague resemblance to the cartoon character and also as the home of some excellent scuba diving and snorkelling. The next point of interest as you head south is the small, restored **Bidiya Mosque**, the oldest mosque in the UAE. **Khor Fakkan** is next, notable for its dramatic setting and busy harbour. **Fujairah** is the largest town on the itinerary, but there's little of interest apart from the museum, which has information about the **Al-Bithnah** (13km back towards Masafi) archaeological sites that are worth a stop.

INFORMATION

130km east of Dubai, travelling time 90 minutes

- 🚗 take Emirates Hwy (E11) towards Sharjah and then the direction of Al-Dhaid (E88); from Masafi you can head north to Dibba or south to Fujairah
- 🖥 www.fujairahmunc.gov.ae

Fort at Al-Bithnah archaeological site (below)

Al-Ain & Buraimi (1, B5)

A trip to these two towns will satisfy that 'oasis in the desert' craving that staying in Dubai can't sate. The towns lie within the Buraimi Oasis, with the UAE–Oman border snaking through the collection of interconnected oases. As well as being a colourful garden city, Al-

INFORMATION

160km southeast of Dubai, travelling time 90 minutes

- 🚗 head south along Sheikh Zayed Rd (E11), take the Al-Ain (E66) exit near Nad al-Sheeba; this Emirates Hwy goes all the way to Al-Ain
- 🖥 www.alain.gov.ae

The ancient burial chamber in the archaeological site at Hili, Al-Ain (opposite)

Ain has some date-palm plantations, forts, a couple of museums and a camel-and-livestock market to explore. Head up to Jebel Hafeet and gaze, Lawrence of Arabia style, at the beginnings of the Empty Quarter.

Abu Dhabi (1, A5)

Relaxed but reserved, the affluent city of Abu Dhabi is in many ways the antithesis of Dubai. Still happily funded by its oil wealth, it doesn't chase the tourist dollar as hard as Dubai. Changes may be afoot, however, with the new and extravagant Arabian-themed **Emirates Palace Hotel** (☎ 02-690 9000; www.kempinski.com; Corniche Rd) located on Abu Dhabi's revamped corniche (waterfront). Abu Dhabi is justifiably proud of its **Cultural Foundation**, with its film festival, musical performances and art exhibitions. The nearby **Qasr Al-Husn** or White Fort was the traditional home of Abu Dhabi's rulers, but is now open to the public. On the way back to Dubai, the **Heritage Village** offers glimpses of Abu Dhabi's traditional Bedouin life.

Abu Dhabi's Cultural Foundation (right) and Etisalat Tower

IINFORMATION
150km southwest of Dubai, travelling time 90 minutes
- 🚌 head south along Sheikh Zayed Rd (E11) and wave to the speed cameras

ORGANISED TOURS

For information about desert safari tours, see p18.

Bus Tours

Big Bus Company (5, E2)
These open-topped London double-decker buses ply two well-chosen routes (city and beach) with 21 stops – you can get off and on at your leisure. The buses leave regularly from Wafi City with a running commentary in English, and free museum entry and other discounts are inclusive. Great for those on a stopover.
☎ 324 4187 🖳 www .bigbustours.com ⊠ Wafi Centre, Bur Dubai 💲 adult/ child/family Dh120/75/315 🕒 9am-5pm

Wonder Bus Tours (2, B3)
One of Dubai's more surreal sights (that's saying something!) awaits you at the BurJuman Centre with the amphibious Wonder Bus. Twice a day up to 44 passengers take the plunge on this two-hour tour that starts on dry land, and travels up and down Dubai Creek.
☎ 359 5656 🖳 www .wonderbusdubai.com

⊠ BurJuman Centre, Bur Dubai 💲 adult/child/family Dh115/75/350 🕒 vary (depends on tide)

City Tours

Arabian Adventures (5, D2)
Owned by Emirates Airlines, Arabian Adventures has a range of excellent tours, such as its half-day city tour, including Jumeirah Rd, the Jumeirah Mosque, the Dubai Museum and the Gold and Spice Souqs in Deira.
☎ 343 9966 🖳 www .arabian-adventures.com ⊠ Emirates Holidays Bldg, Interchange No 2, Sheikh Zayed Rd 💲 varies 🕒 afternoon, time varies

Net Tours & Travels (2, E5)
The four-hour city-tour route starts at Jumeirah Mosque, taking in the Creek, Bastakia, Dubai Museum and the textile market, then an *abra* across the Creek to the Deira Spice and Gold Souqs. It also does a shopping tour.
☎ 266 8661 🖳 www.net toursdubai.com ⊠ Al-Bakhit Centre, Abu Baker al-Siddiq Rd, Hor al-Anz 💲 Dh95 🕒 8.30am/3.30pm

Cruises

Creekside Leisure (2, D4)
With plenty of scheduled cruise times, these one-hour guided tours by *dhow* are a convenient way to get a great overview of the Creek's sights. Also on offer is a great (licensed) dinner cruise with belly dancer.
☎ 336 8407 ⊠ departs in front of the Dubai Municipality building 💲 *dhow* cruise Dh35, dinner cruise Dh175 🕒 11.30am, 1.30pm, 3.30pm, 5.30pm, dinner cruise 8.30-10.30pm

Danat Dubai Cruises (2, C3)
Take the sundowner cruise that goes past the Heritage district before entering the Gulf for sunset. It also offers dinner cruises and transfers.
☎ 351 1117 ⊠ Al-Seef Rd, Bur Dubai 💲 sundowner cruise adult/child Dh65/45 🕒 sundowner cruise boards 5pm, returns 6.30pm

Desert Rangers
The dinner cruise offered is in a classic old *dhow* and takes in all the best of the Creek's architecture and history.
☎ 340 2408 🖳 www .desertrangers.com 💲 adult/child Dh230/160

GO-GODOLPHIN

Lovers of all things equine shouldn't miss the opportunity to take the stable tour at the Nad al-Sheba Club (5, D3). After watching the beautiful thoroughbreds go through their morning training, there's a guided tour around the stables – one of the world's best training facilities. A full English breakfast is followed by a visit to the grandstands and the Godolphin Gallery, which highlights the achievements of Sheikh Mohammed's stable. There's an impressive trophy collection – just don't mention the (current) lack of a Melbourne Cup – something the overachieving Sheikh is desperate to rectify!
☎ 336 3666 🖳 www.nadalshebaclub.com ⊠ Nad al-Sheba district, 5km southeast of Dubai centre 💲 adult/child Dh140/70 💲 Sat, Mon, Wed Sep-Jun

Shopping

Shopping is a ritual for Emiratis, but in Dubai they've taken it to a sublime level. As much a daily event as dinner, it's taken as seriously as eating. Elegant Dubai women, designer *shaylas* dripping with Swarovski crystals hanging loosely around their heads, treat a trip to Chanel as their burka-wearing mothers might a visit to the spice souq. When shopping, they take their time, closely examine the product, consider its quality, and when they're ready to buy…always ask for a discount. The local men are no different, whether buying a PDA or a Porsche, they follow age-old techniques their fathers applied at the camel souq or stock market.

Dubai or not Dubai? BurJuman Centre (p38)

Most shops are open from 10am to 10pm (some close in the afternoon) and malls provide respite from the heat, but evenings are the popular time to shop. People shop late (see p39). Emiratis and expats shop the souqs, malls and streets. They may go from buying frankincense in the spice souq to a marble-floored mall. Enjoy the experience: you can be scouring souqs for antique coffee pots while keeping your eyes peeled for discounted digital cameras. Conversely, you might head to Deira City Centre for spicy oriental perfumes as much as you might for a Plug-Ins sale. Dubai is a postmodern city, and the old and new, traditional and modern are currently in comfortable juxtaposition – make the most of it while you can.

While the lack of taxes and duties (and relatively cheap shipping) ensure you're paying less than elsewhere, no matter where you shop, do as the locals do: always ask for a discount.

HOT SHOPPING AREAS
While most shoppers head to the souqs or malls, Dubai has a number of bustling shopping areas.
- Khalid bin al-Waleed Road, Bur Dubai (2, B2-B3) – Known also as Computer St, shops sell hardware, software, laptops, personal organisers and computer accessories
- Al-Dhiyafah Road, Satwa (3, E2) – *sheesha* pipes, books, mobile phones, Lebanese sweets, and cheap tasty Middle East restaurants when you need to refuel
- Al-Fahidi Street, Bur Dubai (2, B2) – electronics, digital cameras, textiles, tailors and cheap luggage
- Al-Hisn Street & 73 Street, Bur Dubai (2, B2) – sari shops, sequinned slippers, cheap Asian hippy clothes, Bollywood music and movies, and Indian snack shops
- Al-Rigga Road, Deira (2, E3-E4) – Al-Ghurair City mall, discount gift stores, *sheesha* pipes, Iranian and Syrian sweet shops, and outdoor and fast-food restaurants
- Al-Satwa Road (off Al-Dhiyafah Road), Satwa (3, D2-E2) – cheap fabrics, clothes, shoes, luggage and Indian sweet shops
- Sheikh Zayed Road (3, C3-D3) – designer clothes, jewellery, shoes and fine carpets in upmarket hotel arcades, such as Emirates Towers Shopping Blvd, and stylish cafés and *sheesha* spots to rest up

SHOPPING MALLS

BurJuman Centre (2, B3)
Following a stylish make-over, BurJuman is the most glamorous mall in Dubai and a more fitting address for its floors of exclusive shops stocking everything from haute couture (Dior, Lacroix, Ungaro, Kenzo) to more affordable designers (Etro, Moschino), elegant jewellery (Tiffany, Rivoli, Cartier), Saks Fifth Avenue, independent boutiques and cafés.
☎ 352 0222 ✉ cnr Khalid bin al-Waleed & Sheikh Khalifa bin Zayed Rds, Bur Dubai ⏰ 10am-10pm Sat-Thu, 2-10pm Fri

Deira City Centre (2, D6)
Despite openings of bigger, brighter and more bizarre malls (that's you, Ibn Battuta, p30), this remains Dubai's most popular with the widest range of shops, the best bookshop (Magrudys) and arcades dedicated to jewellery, electronics, carpets, crafts and souvenirs. There's a Carrefour supermarket, cafés, food courts,

cinemas and entertainment for kids.
☎ 295 1010 ✉ Al-Garhoud Rd, Deira ⏰ 10am-10pm

Mercato Mall (3, B2)
The only things Italian about Mercato are the mall's cheesy Florentine-cum-Venetian architecture and the notable Bella Donna (p54) restaurant. You'll find the usual range of brands like Bershka, Mango and Promod; shoes, cosmetics and accessories; cinemas; and cafés well-positioned for people-watching in the light-filled courtyards.
☎ 344 4161 ✉ Mercato Mall, Jumeirah Rd, Jumeirah ⏰ 10am-10pm Thu-Sat, 2-10pm Fri

Wafi City Mall (5, E2)
The most elegant shopping centre before BurJuman's revamp, this Egyptian-themed mall is good for designer clothes, shoes, jewellery, accessories and gifts. Its pyramids house some of Dubai's best restaurants, cafés and bars, a fitness centre and spa.
☎ 324 4555 ✉ Al-Qataiyat Rd, near Al-Garhoud Bridge,

Three wishes: Mercato (left)

Bur Dubai ⏰ 10am-10pm Sat-Thu, 2-10pm Fri

SOUQS

Bur Dubai Souq (2, C2)
Arabian 'antiques', kitsch souvenirs and curios can be found among the scores of textile shops, clothes and toys, in this breezy restored waterfront souq. Buy incense, bindis, psychedelic images of Hindu gods and religious trinkets in the narrow lane between the Hindu temples.
✉ btwn Bur Dubai waterfront & Al-Fahidi St, Bur Dubai

Deira Covered Souq & Naif Souq (2, D2)
Similar in content and style, these souqs are most fun at night when you can join Emiratis bargaining for everything from cheap clothes, fake Dior *shaylas* and children's toys at Naif Souq, to household goods, textiles and plastics at Covered Souq.
✉ Covered Souq btwn Al-Sabkha Rd, 67 St & Naif Rd, Deira; Naif Souq btwn Naif South St, 9a St & Deira St, Deira

MALL CULTURE

Much like town centres in other cities, Dubai's malls give travellers a glimpse into its social life and provide an opportunity to mix with locals. Maligned elsewhere, malls make sense in the often stifling heat of Dubai. Their central 'courtyards', with fountain, entertainment stage and souvenir-laden barrows, are like village squares. Older people sit at a café watching the world go by while younger ones send text messages to each other as they promenade. The newest mall, **Ibn Battuta** (see p30), takes the concept to the extreme, with specialised shopping 'streets' resembling market places in 14th-century Andalusia, Tunisia, Egypt, Persia, India and China. Tunisia even has a starry sky for moonlit promenades.

Deira Gold Souq (2, C1)
Head here at night when the gold gleams and gems shine brightest. The covered lanes are crowded with jewellery shoppers out to bargain. Shops selling Arabian perfume, traditional *kandouras* (casual shirt-dresses), Omani hats and belly-dancing costumes line the nearby streets.
✉ Sikkat al-Khail St, btwn Souq Deira & Old Baladiya Sts, Deira

Deira Spice Souq (Old Souq) (2, C2)
Follow your nose to the pungent aromas of the covered alleys of the Spice Souq opposite Deira waterfront. Friendly traders will offer you nuts, spices and dried fruit to try. Saffron, frankincense, henna and rosewater are the best buys. The surrounding narrow streets of Deira Old Souq are worth exploring for the perfumes, *sheesha* pipes and textiles.
✉ btwn Deira waterfront, Al-Abra & Old Baladiya Sts, Deira

Karama Souq (2, A5)
Along with fake designer bags, watches, DVDs, sporting goods and teenage street gear, this is the place to come for cheap handicrafts and kitsch souvenirs, such as Saddam Hussein cigarette lighters, Burj Al Arab paperweights and wooden 'Russian' dolls painted as Emirati nationals.
✉ 18B St, btwn 33B & 45B Sts, Karama, Bur Dubai

Souq Madinat Jumeirah (4, C1)
While prices are higher in the 'antique' and handicrafts stores in this contemporary

LATE-NIGHT SHOPPING
Dubai is at its best at night and locals head out to shop around 8pm and stay out until 10pm. Malls generally open 10am to 10pm daily, except Friday when they open around 2pm. While the chaos of the souqs makes them appealing, there's no centre management so no set hours. Generally, they are open from Saturday to Thursday 10am to 1pm, reopening around 4pm or 5pm until 10pm. Most are shut on Friday, opening Friday evening. It's best to do as the locals do and shop late. That means eating late, but what are days for if not dozing on the beach?

recreation of an old Arabian souq, the quality is better and shopping hassle-free. The excellent restaurants, cafés and bars, awesome architecture, waterfront views and air conditioning are additional incentives.
✉ Madinat Jumeirah, Al-Sufouh Rd, Jumeirah
☾ 10am-11pm

ELECTRONICS

Carrefour (p46) is worth a visit to compare electronics prices before buying and **Virgin Megastore** (p45) also stocks a decent range of iPods and other Apple products.

Al-Ain Shopping Centre (2, B3)
This mall, devoted to computer and electronics, is jam-packed with small

shops that sell every kind of computer hardware, software and accessories conceivable and a decent range of digital cameras and other electronics.
☎ 351 6914 ✉ Al-Mankhool Rd, Bur Dubai
☾ 10am-2.30pm & 4.30-10pm Sat-Thu, 4.30-10pm Fri

Plug-Ins (2, D6)
By far the most expansive range of products in town, from the teensiest digital cameras to professional DV cameras, you'll have ample choice here. Browse for home cinemas and flat-screen TVs, MP3 players and state-of-the-art sound systems, to PCs and personal organisers; Plug-Ins has it all and generally at the lowest prices.
☎ 295 0404 ✉ Deira City Centre, Al-Garhoud Rd, Deira
☾ 10am-10pm Sat-Thu, 2-10pm Fri

BARGAINING 101

Relished by some, tedious for others, bargaining in souqs and small stores can get you a 20% to 50% discount if you're prepared to haggle patiently. Do as the locals do: when given a price, offer 50% less. Respond to the salesperson's reaction, adjusting your offer accordingly. As the process draws to an end, ask for their final and best price. If they agree to your offer, pay up – offering a lower figure or leaving is considered impolite. Bargaining in a mall is acceptable in carpet, computer and electronics stores. Perfume and cosmetics stores sometimes also offer discounts.

CLOTHING & ACCESSORIES

Amzaan (5, E2)
Young Maisa al-Qassimi's boutique has been a breath of fresh air for the local fashion scene with its funky design – curtains of chains, Lomo wallpaper – and spirited labels Antik Batik, Religion Cycle, Fidel, Pause and Faust. Also stocks local brand Pink Sushi's fantastic bags made from checked *gutras* (men's headdresses) and decorated with Bedouin jewellery.
☎ 324 6754 ✉ Wafi City Mall, Al-Qataiyat Rd, near Al-Garhoud Bridge, Bur Dubai ⏰ 10am-10pm Sat-Thu, 2-10pm Fri

Fae (2, C2)
The historic wind-tower house and nondescript entrance give no hint of the glamour that is to be found inside. The only boutique outside India where the country's most interesting women's designers can be found, Fae's racks hang heavy with sequinned tops, appliqué tees and glittery gowns from Satya Paul, Ritu Kumar, Rohit Bai, Asha Ridanldi, Kavita Bhartiya and more.
☎ 353 9695 ✉ Villa 15-B Bastakia, Bur Dubai ⏰ 10am-9pm Sat-Thu

Five Green (2, B5)
This retail store, gallery and performance space, stocks unisex street-style labels you won't see elsewhere in Dubai: XLarge; BoxFresh; GSUS; Paul Frank and Upper Playground; plus Dubai-based designers Saadia Zahid, Mona Ibrahim, chadiyo and Essa; cool urban accessories; retro Lomo cameras; and magazines by indie publishers.
☎ 336 4100 ✉ Aroma Garden Café Bldg, Oud Metha Rd, Bur Dubai ⏰ 10am-11pm Sat-Thu, 4-11pm Fri

Jimmy Choo (3, D3)
The shoes that found fame on the feet of sexy sitcom stars are now a household name in Dubai. Recline on the chaise longue at the fabulous flagship store so you can see how these shoes transform those calves of yours.
☎ 330 0404 ✉ Emirates Towers Shopping Blvd, Sheikh Zayed Rd ⏰ 10am-10pm Sat-Thu, 4-10pm Fri

Kenneth Cole (2, B3)
While Kenneth Cole's exquisitely tailored clothes, leather bags, shoes and belts may scream New York they probably can't be had elsewhere for as little as they can during Dubai sales when prices drop tremendously.
☎ 4355 5872 ✉ BurJuman Centre, Sheikh Khalifa bin Zayed Rd, Bur Dubai ⏰ 10am-10pm Sat-Thu, 2-10pm Fri

Laundry by Shelli Segal (2, B3)
If you rapture over flowing dresses embellished with Indian-inspired embroidery, antique beadwork on crinkly chiffon, strapless summery dresses, or halter tops with hanky hems, then you'll love Laundry's feminine style. The gorgeous Dubai shop is one of a few outside North America.
☎ 4355 8920 ✉ BurJuman Centre, Sheikh Khalifa bin Zayed Rd, Bur Dubai ⏰ 10am-10pm Sat-Thu, 2-10pm Fri

Praias (2, B3)
Forget your swimsuit? Then look no further than Praias (beach in Portuguese) and its racks of vibrant Brazilian bikinis decorated with beads, shells and appliqué. The teensy sizes may be daring for Dubai but, once you have these on, you won't want to leave your hotel poolside.
☎ 4351 1338 ✉ BurJuman Centre, Sheikh Khalifa bin Zayed Rd, Bur Dubai ⏱ 10am-10pm Sat-Thu, 2-10pm Fri

Saks Fifth Avenue (2, B3)
This new BurJuman resident has been warmly welcomed, with tenants Oscar de la Renta, Jean Paul Gaultier, Galliano, Elie Saab, Marc Jacobs, Pucci, and Diane Von Furstenberg. It also has Vera Wang wedding gowns, Plein Sud jeans, sexy Agent Provocateur lingerie, a designer children's section and cosmetics brands Stephane Marais, Smashbox, By Terry and Gaultier for Men – who wouldn't be happy?
☎ 4355 8920 ✉ BurJuman Centre, Sheikh Khalifa bin Zayed Rd, Bur Dubai ⏱ 10am-10pm Sat-Thu, 2-10pm Fri

Sauce (3, C1)
One of only a few independent boutiques in Dubai, this cool shop stocks quirky and idiosyncratic women's labels like Sass and Bide, Third Millennium, Tata-Naka, Sara Berman, Willow, Studd, Dice Kayek and Citizens of Humanity jeans, along with unique accessories, home and design objects.
☎ 344 7270 ✉ Village Mall, Jumeirah Rd, Jumeirah ⏱ 10am-10pm Sat-Thu, 4.30-10pm Fri

Villa Moda (3, D3)
The funky futuristic *2001: A Space Odyssey* interior is reason enough to visit Kuwait 'Sheikh of Chic', Majed al-Sabah's one-stop designer shop. That its curvy white capsulelike boutiques provide homes to the hottest fashion houses – Alexander McQueen, Easton Pearson, Stella McCartney, Chloe, Missoni, Miu Miu, Prada, Marni and more – is an bonus.
☎ 330 4555 ✉ Emirates Towers Shopping Blvd, Sheikh Zayed Rd ⏱ 10am-10pm Sat-Thu, 4-10pm Fri

Whistles (2, B3)
Only available in the UK and Middle East, the whimsical women's fashion of Whistles is hard to resist, with recent collections combining Euro peasant and wild gypsy styles to produce an eclectic range of colourful kaftans and beach ponchos, ruffled skirts and tops trimmed with crochet.
☎ 351 5070 ✉ BurJuman Centre, Sheikh Khalifa bin Zayed Rd, Bur Dubai ⏱ 10am-10pm Sat-Thu, 2-10pm Fri

Women's Secret (2, D6)
Each affordable lingerie, swimwear and sleepwear range from this Spanish franchise reflects a melting pot of cultures and styles, with the latest offerings featuring funky Mexican, Spanish, Japanese and Hawaiian designs.
☎ 295 9665 ✉ Deira City Centre, Al-Garhoud Rd, Deira ⏱ 10am-10pm

DUTY-FREE SHOPPING
Duty-free shopping in the UAE doesn't necessarily offer the discounts it does in other countries because the place is blissfully tax-free. Prices are low but always shop around, compare prices and ask for discounts. While the souqs may be cheaper, consider paying the extra dirhams for the international warranties provided in the more respectable retail stores in malls. If you run out of time, Dubai Duty Free's prices are comparable and the airport shops are open 24 hours.

GOING FOR GOLD

As with most things bought in Dubai, there's room to bargain when buying gold, so shop around to get the price down. While gold is sold by weight, the cost of gold jewellery varies depending on whether it's hand-crafted or machine-made. The greater the grade of gold the more expensive the product, and you can be confident that if a salesperson tells you a piece is 22 carat, it is – strict authenticity laws can quickly put a gold trader out of business.

GOLD & JEWELLERY

Azza Fahmy Jewellery (3, D3)

Egyptian Azza Fahmy's stunning jewellery draws on Islamic and Arab traditions, combining classical Arabic poetry and Islamic wisdom in fine calligraphy, with gemstones, beads, and motifs and elements from different ages and civilisations.
☎ 330 0340 ✉ Emirates Towers Shopping Blvd, Sheikh Zayed Rd ⏱ 10am-10pm Sat-Thu, 4-10pm Fri

Damas (2, D6)

The largest and most reliable jewellery retailer in the

Gold: room to bargain

region, Damas has branches all over the city. While it specialises in gold, diamonds, pearls and watches in styles to suit all tastes, the elaborate and intricate Arab- and Indian-influenced pieces are also magnificent.
☎ 295 3848 ✉ Deira City Centre, Al-Garhoud Rd, Deira ⏱ 10am-10pm

Gold & Diamond Park (4, C2)

This air-conditioned centre houses more than a hundred jewellery retailers and manufacturers in a purpose-built Arabian-style shopping centre. Here you'll find finely crafted traditional and contemporary jewellery, gold, pearls and diamonds, and you can commission your own designs.
☎ 347 7788 ✉ Sheikh Zayed Rd, near Interchange No 4 ⏱ 10am-10pm Sat-Thu, 4-10pm Fri

Tiffany & Co. (2, B3)

Internationally renowned for its clean and classical designs and captivating diamond rings, Tiffany's more contemporary sterling silver jewellery, such as the feather pendant, has a lot more style.
☎ 359 0101 ✉ BurJuman Centre, Sheikh Khalifa

bin Zayed Rd, Bur Dubai ⏱ 10am-10pm Sat-Thu, 2-10pm Fri

PERFUMES & COSMETICS

Ajmal (2, D6)

In pre–air conditioning days Emirati women used strong, spicy *attar* (Arabic perfume) to disguise the smell of perspiration. Local ladies still seem to prefer the headier scents (as you'll notice when you pass an Emirati woman), and Ajmal is nearly always crowded with women in elegant burkas trying and buying the jewel-encrusted bottles of exotic oils and *attars*.
☎ 295 3580 ✉ Deira City Centre, Al-Garhoud Rd, Deira ⏱ 10am-10pm

Faces (2, B3)

Local and expat women will need to find other excuses to visit Paris these days, as Faces stocks a range of those brilliant brands that were previously impossible to get in Dubai: Serge Lutens, L'Artisan Parfumer, Pout, Benefit, Priorities, Annick Goutal and L'Erbolario.
☎ 352 1441 ✉ BurJuman Centre, Sheikh Khalifa bin Zayed Rd, Bur Dubai ⏱ 10am-10pm Thu-Sat, 2-10pm Fri

Mikyajy (2, D6)

Local girls eagerly await the launch of any new product from Mikyajy. Produced to meet the make-up needs of Middle East gals, this Gulf brand's popularity is partly due to its focus on vibrant colours. 'Turquoise', for

The ritual of shopping

instance, is a turquoise make-up tin containing mascara, eyeshadow, eyeliner, eye crayon and shadow pencil in...you guessed it – turquoise!

☎ 295 7844 ✉ Deira City Centre, Al-Garhoud Rd, Deira ☾ 10am-10pm Sat-Thu, 2-10pm Fri

Paris Gallery (2, D6)
This perfume and cosmetics chain has the widest range of international products in Dubai. Although the sales staff are pushy, they give good discounts, and due to ongoing promotions there's always something extra that's dropped into your shopping bag.

☎ 294 1111 ✉ Deira City Centre, Al-Garhoud Rd, Deira ☾ 10am-10pm

Rituals (2, D6)
Turning routines into meaningful rituals is the purpose of these exquisite natural products. Learn to enjoy doing dishes with Ray of Light (yuzu and tea-tree oil) washing-up liquid, enliven your laundering with Lotus Mist, or linger in a luscious bath with Magic Milk. Sincere aim or just good marketing, it works for us!

☎ 294 1432 ✉ Deira City Centre, Al-Garhoud Rd, Deira ☾ 10am-10pm

CARPETS & TEXTILES

Aminian Persian Carpets (2, D6)
Established in Iran in 1936, this shop imports a wide range of high-quality rugs from across the region, from intricately patterned silk carpets favoured by collectors to the increasingly popular tribal kilims with contemporary geometric designs.

☎ 295 5379 ✉ Deira City Centre, Al-Garhoud Rd, Deira ☾ 10am-10pm Sat-Thu, 2-10pm Fri

Persian Carpet House & Antiques (3, B1)
One of the best sources of hand-woven carpets and rugs, the Persian Carpet

House stocks a wide variety of exquisite carpets from Iran, India Kashmir, Pakistan and Afghanistan, as well as a small range from Turkey, China and Russia; it also stocks Oriental 'antiques' and curios.

☎ 345 6687 ✉ Mercato Mall, Jumeirah Rd, Jumeirah ☾ 10am-10pm Thu-Sat, 2-10pm Fri

Pride of Kashmir (2, D6)
Specialists in fine carpets from Kashmir, Afghanistan, Pakistan and Iran, this shop also stocks a wonderful range of rich embroidered and sequinned textiles – perfect as wall hangings, throws and tablecloths – along with genuine pashmina shawls, bedspreads with fine beading, and velvet and silk cushions.

☎ 295 1010 ✉ Deira City Centre, Al-Garhoud Rd, Deira ☾ 10am-10pm

ART, CRAFTS & SOUVENIRS

Al-Jaber Gallery (2, D6)
This cluttered shop has the largest selection of Arabian souvenirs, traditional handicrafts and Oriental 'antiques' around. The framed *khanjars* (daggers) and Omani silver jewellery are very popular,

---

SHOPPING ITINERARY FOR A SHOPAHOLICS' STOPOVER:

Start at **Deira City Centre** (p38) to get your bearings on what Dubai has to offer and start bargaining for a carpet. Take a taxi to **BurJuman** (p38) for **Saks Fifth Avenue** (p41) and other seductive boutiques, then to Emirates Towers Shopping Blvd for **Villa Moda** (p41), **Azza Fahmy** (opposite) and **Jimmy Choo** (p40). Refuel at the **Noodle House** (p53). Head down the beach to **Souq Madinat Jumeirah** (p39), before bargaining at the real souqs. Start with **Bur Dubai Souq** (p38) then take an *abra* to the Deira souqs. Be sure to return to Deira City Centre by 10pm to make a final offer on that carpet!

THE ART OF CARPET BUYING

Patience, persistence and research are essential. Visit a number of shops and compare the quality and prices. Flip the corner of the rug over – the more knots per square inch, the greater the quality. Examine the design – the more intricate the detail, the more expensive it will be. Silk carpets are more valuable than wool, and natural dyes more expensive than artificial. Antique rugs are naturally dyed and appear slightly faded (this isn't a flaw). Bargain hard: feign indecisiveness over several carpets and you'll be offered a discount for two. Even better, take a rug-buying friend and get further discounts. Lastly, don't feel obliged to buy just because 20 carpets have been unrolled – along with the tea, this is part of the ritual.

but henna kits and *sheesha* pipes often make more special souvenirs, as you'll probably try both of these in Dubai.

☎ 295 1010 ✉ Deira City Centre, Al-Garhoud Rd, Deira ⏰ 10am-10pm

Allah Din Shoes (2, C2)

Although many souvenir shops now stock sequinned slippers and fantastic gold-threaded, embroidered curly-toed Aladdin shoes from Pakistan and Afghanistan, this small outdoor stall at the *abra* dock was the first. It's still the best for quality and variety.

☎ 050 515 4351 ✉ Dubai Old Souq abra station, Bur Dubai ⏰ 10am-10pm Sat-Thu, 4-10pm Fri

Al-Orooba Oriental (2, B3)

One of the few stores to stock authentic antiques and quality collectables in Dubai, with an impressive selection of Bedouin jewellery, old *khanjars*, intricately patterned coffee pots and trays, beautiful ceramics, miniature Persian paintings and prayer beads.

☎ 351 0919 ✉ BurJuman Centre, Bur Dubai ⏰ 10am-10pm Sat-Thu, 2-10pm Fri

Camel Company (4, C1)

Your one-stop camel shop in Dubai stocks cute camels in every conceivable shape, texture and form – fluffy camels in Hawaiian shirts and shorts or tutus, and plush ones that are so huggable you won't

want to let them go. There are also camel-themed notebooks, mouse-pads, greeting cards, stationery, T-shirts, coffee mugs and more.

☎ 368 6048 ✉ Souq Madinat Jumeirah, Al-Sufouh Rd, Jumeirah ⏰ 10am-11pm

Gallery One Fine Art Photographs (4, C1)

These stunning framed photographs of Dubai, its wind-tower architecture, creek activity, street life, and Madinat Jumeirah itself, come in colour and black-and-white, and make great mementos.

☎ 368 6055 ✉ Souq Madinat Jumeirah, Al-Sufouh Rd, Jumeirah ⏰ 10am-11pm

Gifts & Souvenirs (2, A5)

Out of the dozens of souvenir shops in Karama Souq, this one has the widest range and best quality – brass coffee pots, Aladdin lamps, colourful *kandouras*, *gutra*-and-*agal* sets, incense kits with frankincense, clay burners and coal – all great gifts.

☎ 337 7884 ✉ Karama Souq, Karama ⏰ 9am-10.30pm Sat-Thu, 9-11am & 4-10.30pm Fri

Showcase Antiques, Art & Frames (4, D1)

This three-storey villa's high-quality collectables and antiques come with certificates of authenticity. Along with antique *khanjars*, firearms, coffee pots and wooden chests, there are colourful costumes and some wonderful Bedouin jewellery.

☎ 348 8797 ✉ Jumeirah Rd, Umm Suqeim ⏰ 10am-1pm & 4-8pm Sat-Thu, 4-8pm Fri

TOP FIVE DUBAI READS

- *Dubai Tales* – Mohammad Al-Murr
- *Father of Dubai: Sheikh Rashid bin Saeed Al-Maktoum* – Graeme Wilson
- *Dubai Life and Times: Through the Lens of Noor Ali Rashid* – Noor Ali Rashid
- *The Wells of Memory, An Autobiography* – Easa Saleh Al-Gurg
- *Dubai, A Collection of Mid-twentieth Century Photographs* – Ronald Codrai

MUSIC & BOOKS

Book Corner (2, E3)
The largest bookshop in Dubai, Book Corner has an enormous selection of books in both Arabic and English. The travel section is the most extensive in Dubai, stocking Lonely Planet guides and almost every other brand on the market, along with phrase books, travel documentary videos, maps and atlases.
☎ 223 2333 ✉ Al-Ghurair City, cnr Al-Rigga & Omar ibn al-Khattab Rds, Deira ⏰ 9am-1pm & 5-10pm Sat-Thu, 5-10pm Fri

Magrudy's (2, D6)
Magrudy's has the best range of English-language material in the city, as well as glossy coffee-table books on Dubai, texts on Middle East history, politics and society, the latest best sellers, classics and general fiction. It excels in nonfiction areas of travel, cooking and interior design. The magazine section could be better.
☎ 295 7744 ✉ Deira City Centre, Al-Garhoud Rd, Deira ⏰ 10am-10pm

Ohm Records (2, B4)
One of the best things to happen to Dubai's music scene, this was the first shop to carry vinyl, along with DJ gear, and a serious selection

of house, trance, drum and bass and trip hop.
☎ 397 3728 ✉ Sheikh Khalifa bin Zayed Rd, opposite BurJuman Centre, Bur Dubai ⏰ 2-10pm

Virgin Megastore (2, D6)
Take full advantage of Virgin's listening stands to select your musical souvenirs from the largest offering of Arabian music, ranging from hip lounge, chill-out music and cool fusion, to more traditional oud (Arabian lute) and folk music, popular Emirati singers and Lebanese pop stars. There's also a decent selection of Arabian DVDs and MP3 players.
☎ 295 8599 ✉ Deira City Centre, Al-Garhoud Rd, Deira ⏰ 10am-10pm

FOOD & DRINK

Bateel (2, B3)
Applying traditional European chocolate-making techniques to quality local dates, Bateel produces delicious date chocolates, truffles, marzipan and nougat, along with date jams and a sparkling date drink! Offering dates is intrinsic to traditional Arabian hospitality, but now Emiratis offer Bateel's silver platters and luxuriously gift-wrapped boxes for Eids, birthdays and other celebrations.
☎ 355 2853 ✉ BurJuman Centre, cnr Khalid bin al-Waleed & Sheikh Khalifa bin Zayed Rds, Bur Dubai ⏰ 10am-10pm Sat-Thu, 2-10pm Fri

DUBAI'S SHOPPING FESTIVALS

Started as a way to promote retail trade in Dubai, the Dubai Shopping Festival (www.mydsf.com), held from January to February, brings in tourists from around the world. The great weather, myriad festival events, nightly fireworks and retail sales are key attractions, but the best fun is the kitsch Global Village. There's nothing quite like choosing between Chinese opera and whirling dervishes, after some Bavarian food on your way to buying some Tunisian pottery.

Flush with the success of the Shopping Festival, Dubai also hosts Dubai Summer Surprises. Designed to attract tourists during the traditionally lean summer period of July and August, it's a very kids-oriented festival, with an inexplicably popular mascot, Modhesh, who resembles…a bright yellow airbed foot pump.

TOP FIVE SOUVENIR FOODS

• Iranian caviar – the cheapest place outside Iran to buy it
• Al Jazeera Arabic coffee – especially for the veiled lady on the tin
• Cardamom-flavoured condensed milk – delicious with coffee or tea
• Rose syrup – try it with soda water, in milkshakes or on ice cream
• Zaatar & sumach – the herb and spice most used locally

Carrefour (2, D6)

Perpetually crowded Carrefour has the widest selection of international products of any Dubai supermarket; it also has delicious fresh bread, Arabian sweets and pastries, an awesome deli counter with barrels of delicious Middle East olives, and cheeses from around the globe – perfect provisions for a waterside picnic!
☎ 295 1600 ✉ Deira City Centre, Al-Garhoud Rd, Deira ⏰ 9am-midnight Sat-Thu, 10am-midnight Fri

Caviar Classic (4, C1)

Connoisseurs can take advantage of Dubai's low

prices and indulge their taste buds with Royal Beluga, which is Dh375 for 50g, or Dh7500 (US$2080) a kilogram. The more affordable Sevruga is a mere Dh150 for 50g, or Dh3000 (US$832) a kilogram. Despite the nifty packaging and ice, it won't survive the plane trip home, so savour it with bubbly on the hotel balcony.
☎ 368 6160 ✉ Shop 131, Souq Madinat Jumeirah, Al-Sufouh Rd, Jumeirah ⏰ 10am-11pm

Goodies (5, E2)

This Dubai branch of Lebanon's popular food hall and restaurant simply overflows with barrels of the juiciest olives, the spiciest peppers and the tastiest pickles, along with a range of fresh white cheeses, hummus, *baba ghanooj* and *muttabal*, and tabbouleh, fried *kibbeh* and Lebanese pastries that are made on the premises. Take a seat and eat in or take it away.
☎ 324 4555 ✉ Wafi City Mall, Al-Qataiyat Rd, near Al-Garhoud Bridge, Bur Dubai ⏰ 10am-10pm Sat-Thu, 2-10pm Fri

Organic Foods & Café (3, E2)

The city's first organic supermarket and café boasts the freshest of fruit, vegetables, seafood and meat. It bakes bread on premises, roasts and grinds coffee, offers tastings of delicious Mediterranean olive oils, and stocks an extraordinary range of every organic and gluten-free product imaginable.
☎ 398 9410 ✉ Mankhool Rd, near Satwa Roundabout, Satwa ⏰ 8am-10pm

Panini (5, E2)

This gourmet food store (a Dubai rarity) has the best selection of Italian products in the city – olive oils, balsamic vinegars, truffle paste, pasta sauces, Italian pasta and cheeses – along with Middle East specialities such as Moroccan couscous and basil-infused Argan oil. Fresh bread and pastries are baked in store.
☎ 317 2620 ✉ Grand Hyatt Dubai, Al-Qataiyat Rd, Bur Dubai ⏰ 8am-1am

FOR CHILDREN

Early Learning Centre (2, D6)

If you need to keep the kids amused while travelling or want to buy a toy that won't be discarded in minutes, this educational toy shop specialising in stimulating stuff for kids is just the place.
☎ 295 1548 ✉ Deira City Centre, Al-Garhoud Rd, Deira ⏰ 10am-10pm

Mothercare (2, A6)

From baby carriers and car seats, to cute-as-a-button clothes and plush toys, this

popular shop has everything a parent needs, and it's all extremely affordable. There are a dozen other kids' shops on the same floor at this Lamcy Plaza branch.
☎ 335 9999 ✉ Lamcy Plaza, Oud Metha, Bur Dubai ☾ 10am-10pm

Tape A L'oeil (2, B3)
This wonderful French shop has all kinds of adorable outfits for the little ones, all the way from swimwear and pyjamas to casual gear and formal wear. The clothes may be adult in style but they come in teensy sizes: pretty floral frocks with matching sunhats for her, and khaki long shorts and colourful polo shirts for him.
☎ 352 3223 ✉ BurJuman Centre, cnr Khalid bin al-Waleed & Sheikh Khalifa bin Zayed Rds, Bur Dubai ☾ 10am-10pm Sat-Thu, 2-10pm Fri

TOP FIVE SOUVENIRS
• Iranian carpets and tribal rugs – the best quality and prices outside Iran
• Arabian 'antiques' – traditional *khanjars*, coffee pots and Aladdin lamps
• *Gutra*-and-*agal* sets for him and elegant *shaylas* for her – dress up as Sheikh Jim and Sheikha Jane at home
• Kitsch trinkets – Burj Al Arab paperweights, veiled Arabian woman fridge magnets, mosque alarm clocks
• Arabian music – chill out to fusion beats from the Middle East when you get home

TOP FIVE DUBAI SOUNDS
• *Lemonada, The Arabian Latin Chillout Experience* – Ahmad Ghannoum
• *Blue Bedouin* – Hussain al-Bagali
• *Oryx* – Bashar Abed Rabbo & Dirk Heibel
• *Yaseer Habeeb* – Yaseer Habeeb
• *Now That's What I Call Arabia 8* – Various Artists

SPECIALITY & QUIRKY STORES

Al-Mansoor Audio Video (2, A6)
If you ever doubted that Bollywood rivalled Hollywood in output, then head here. Specialising in Bollywood movies and music, this shop must have the largest range outside India.
☎ 337 1779 ✉ Lamcy Plaza, Oud Metha, Bur Dubai ☾ 10am-10pm

Music Chamber (3, D3)
If you've fallen in love with the sound of the oud and want to try your hand at learning to play one, this specialist musical-instrument shop stocks a good selection of student- to professional-quality ouds. The shop also offers lessons to help you get started.
☎ 331 6416 ✉ Crowne Plaza Shopping Centre, Sheikh Zayed Rd ☾ 10am-11pm Sat-Thu, 5-10pm Fri

Petals (5, E2)
The ceiling of this interior-decorations shop drips with colourful crystal chandeliers, while the floors are cluttered with velvet chaise longues, heavy antique sideboards, baroque tapestry chairs, gilded mirrors and other eccentric pieces. More practical souvenirs include coloured glasses, charming wooden boxes, scented candles and aromatherapy products.
☎ 324 6266 ✉ Wafi City Mall, Al-Qataiyat Rd, near Al-Garhoud Bridge, Bur Dubai ☾ Sat-Thu 10am-10pm, Fri 2-10pm

Rampage (3, C1)
Serving Dubai's burgeoning board-sports scene, Rampage stocks skateboards and accessories as well as skate clothing and beach gear.
☎ 344 7034 ✉ Village Mall, Jumeirah Rd, Jumeirah ☾ 10am-10pm Sat-Thu, 4.30-10pm Fri

Eating

The food and restaurant scene in Dubai is vast – there's everything from cheap street *shwarma* (spit-roasted meat in pita) to haute cuisine in five-star hotels. However, between the two there are copious distinctly mediocre hotel restaurants as well as some real gems. As a rule, hotels are the only establishments blessed with a liquor licence, so if you wish to imbibe with your meal you're going to walk through as many hotel foyers as a travelling salesman.

Just about every type of food you could crave is available in Dubai, but, surprisingly, decent Emirati or Gulf food is hard to find, unless you score an invitation to a local wedding. The main dish at weddings, *khouzi*, consists of a whole roasted lamb or baby camel stuffed with rice and spices. More commonly found in local restaurants is chicken, lamb or shrimp *mashbous*, where the meat is spiced and served with equally spicy rice. Being on the coast, seafood is very popular and the favourite local fish is *hammour*, a tasty member of the groper family.

Restaurant hours are generally from 12.30pm to 3pm and from 7.30pm to midnight, while cafés are usually open from 9am to midnight. Residents generally book the better restaurants for 9pm, whereas for Arabian/Lebanese restaurants with live music, an 11pm reservation is fashionable as the hip-shaking entertainment usually continues until about 3am. For decent hotel restaurants it's best to book a couple of days in advance (especially for weekends) and the modish tables in Dubai may be booked up to a couple of weeks in advance – at least until the next hip eatery opens! Menus are always in English and tipping is not necessarily expected, which goes a long way to explaining the comical 'service' you'll often receive. Most restaurants now have nonsmoking areas and children are welcome almost everywhere except for a couple of the fine-dining establishments.

MEAL COSTS

The pricing symbols used in this chapter indicate the cost of a main course for one person at dinner, excluding drinks. Alcohol adds significantly to these costs; for details see p50.

$	under Dh20
$$	Dh21-40
$$$	Dh41-65
$$$$	over Dh65

DEIRA

Blue Elephant
(5, E2)
Thai $$$$
Along with Benjarong (p53), this represents the most refined Thai dining in town. You might hesitate after seeing the kitsch Thai village that awaits you (hey, this *is* Dubai!), but relax and order the Royal Thai Banquet. Curries are fantastic, but watch the heat – it's the real deal.
☎ 705 4660 ⊠ Al-Bustan Rotana, Casablanca Rd, Al-Garhoud ⏰ noon-3pm & 7-11.30pm Ⓥ

Café Chic
(5, E2)
Fine Dining $$$$
The elegant interior of this restaurant perhaps leads you to expect more than the decent bistro food that's on offer, especially since its menu was put together by two-star chef Michel Rostang. However the excellent wine list and ultrarich chocolate soufflé make up for any shortcomings.
☎ 282 4040 ⊠ Le Meridien Dubai, Airport Rd, Al-Garhoud ⏰ 12.30-2.45pm & 8-11.45pm

Café Havana
(2, D6)
Café $$
Popular with groups of elegant Emirati men, the good coffee here runs a distant second to the people-watching opportunities, making this the best choice to rest up between comparing iPod prices at this uberpopular mall.
☎ 295 5238 ⊠ Deira City Centre, Level II, Al-Garhoud Rd ⏰ 8am-midnight

Casa Mia
(5, E2)
Italian $$$
This fuss-free, authentic Italian trattoria is a long-standing local favourite – and with good reason. Great starters (especially the beef *carpaccio*), fresh pasta and a wood-fired pizza oven means you probably won't have room for the excellent *secondi* (main courses) and desserts.
☎ 702 2506 ⊠ Le Meridien Dubai, Airport Rd, Al-Garhoud ⏰ 12.30-2.45pm & 8-11.30pm Ⓥ

China Club
(2, D3)
Contemporary Chinese $$$
This delicately beautiful restaurant looks fantastic in the evenings (check out the banquet room) and thankfully the food does the interior justice. Stick to the classics – such as the Peking duck – and pray that you get one of the better waiters, as the service here is a little haphazard. The excellent traditional Yum Cha beats other Friday brunches (Friday is 'Sunday' in Dubai) hands down.
☎ 222 7171 ⊠ InterContinental Hotel, Baniyas Rd ⏰ 1-3pm & 8-11pm

Creekside
(2, D4)
Japanese $$$
A no-nonsense Japanese restaurant offering all the expected delights – sushi, sashimi, noodles, tempura and some of the best teppanyaki in town. Friendly and knowledgeable staff will help you work your way through the myriad choices including the decent wine list.
☎ 207 1750 ⊠ Sheraton Dubai Creek, Baniyas Rd ⏰ 12.30-3pm & 6.30pm-midnight

Glasshouse Mediterranean Brasserie
(2, D4)
Modern Mediterranean $$$
The revamp of the Hilton's second restaurant (the other being the excellent Verre, p50) has resulted in what has to be Dubai's best 'by the glass' wine selection as well as a more focussed brasserie menu. Its take on classics such as salad *niçoise* are exemplary, but it's difficult not to take furtive glances over to its more refined sibling across the hotel.
☎ 227 1111 ⊠ Hilton Dubai Creek, Baniyas Rd ⏰ 12.30-3.30pm & 7-11.30pm

Asha's (p51): inventive dishes and informed service

LIQUOR & THE LIBERAL STATE

While Dubai is a Muslim state, alcohol laws allow tourists and (non-Muslim) expats a little alcohol-enhanced happiness. However, you can't buy 'take-away' alcohol in Dubai without a licence and these are issued only to residents, so stock up before coming through customs.

Generally, only hotels are licensed to sell alcohol to be consumed on the premises. A beer or a decent glass of wine costs around Dh18 to Dh24 and wine by the bottle starts at about Dh100. The range and quality of wines is reasonable, but check those corks – there's quite a high spoilage rate in Dubai. All the latest drinking trends are in evidence here – *caipirinhas* (sugarcane-liquor and lime cocktail) and *mojitos* (rum-based cocktail) appear on most lists and the insidious 'alchopops' are popular.

Miyako (2, E1)
Japanese $$$$
After the Hyatt Regency's groovy makeover, Miyako has emerged looking fresh faced. The detailed menu is uniformly good – the sushi and sashimi are first class – and classic dishes such as pork belly are refined and melt-in-your-mouth delicious.
☎ 209 1222 ✉ Hyatt Regency, off Al-Khaleej Rd 🕑 12.30-3pm & 7-11pm

More (5, E2)
Café $$
Chain cafés are the bane of our existence in Dubai (thank you Seattle!), which is why we come to praise More and not complain about its

slightly off-the-tourist-trail location. The menu and décor are eclectic, the all-day breakfast a godsend after a late night, and we wish they'd open one in Jumeirah – we don't care if that makes it a franchise.
☎ 283 0224 ✉ near Welcare Hospital, Al-Garhoud 🕑 7.30am-12.30am

M's Beef Bistro (5, E2)
Steakhouse $$$$
This welcoming American-style steakhouse is a meat-lovers favourite on this side of the Creek. Have it raw (the *carpaccio* and tartare are super), or cooked to order (Béarnaise sauce on the side, thanks) and you're in carnivorous heaven.

Lime Tree Café (p55) cures the homesick blues

A good wine selection and fine service help seal the deal.
☎ 282 4040 ✉ Le Meridien Dubai, Airport Rd, Al-Garhoud 🕑 12.30-2.45pm & 7.30-11.45pm

Shahrzad (2, E1)
Persian $$$$
Shahrzad offers excellent Iranian cuisine and live music with an antique-filled feel of old Persia. As soon as you enter the restaurant the enticing aromas of bread cooked in the traditional *tanour* (oven) and meat kebabs slowly cooking on the open grill will make you hungry. It's a mouthwatering experience
☎ 209 1200 ✉ Hyatt Regency, off Al-Khaleej Rd 🕑 12.30-3.30pm & 7.30-11pm, closed Sat

Verre (2, D4)
Fine Dining $$$$
Dubai's most consistent fine dining experience is still Gordon Ramsay's Verre. We're not sure whether it's the chef's love of food or the staff's fear of the infamous wrath of Ramsay that keeps it special, but who cares when the food is so exceptional? Ramsay's signature

An atmospheric stop on a snoop round the Bastakia Quarter at Basta Art Café (below)

combination of French technique and light touch is followed meticulously, and the restaurant's sommelier is the only one worthy of the title in Dubai.
☎ 212 7551 ✉ Hilton Dubai Creek, Baniyas Rd ✆ 7pm-midnight

YUM! (2, D3)
Noodle Bar $$
This side of the creek's answer to Noodle House (p53), Yum! serves up fine far-Eastern fare fresh from its open kitchen. The *tom kha gai* (chicken and coconut soup) and wok specials such as *char kway teow* (stir-fried noodles) are excellent, but the service can be a tad slow.
☎ 222 7171 ✉ InterContinental Hotel, Baniyas Rd ✆ noon-1am

BUR DUBAI

Antique Bazaar (2, B3)
Indian $$$
While Asha's looks forward, Antique Bazaar, with its lavish interior and traditional menu takes diners on a decidedly nostalgic Indian tour. The food and service are exemplary, but it's not until

the dancer (after 9pm) does her stuff that this welcoming restaurant heads to another dimension.
☎ 397 7444 ✉ Four Points Sheraton, Bank St ✆ 12.30-3pm & 7.30pm-3am Sat-Thu, 7.30pm-3am Fri

Asha's (5, E2)
Contemporary Indian $$$
While the success of Asha's has spawned a few copycats in Dubai, there's more to updating Northern Indian cuisine than halving portions and prettying plates. The contemporary dishes here are inventive, the classics handled with aplomb and the informed service and funky décor make this a class act.
☎ 324 4100 ✉ Pyramids, Wafi City, Al-Qataiyat Rd ✆ 12.30-3.30pm & 7.30pm-2am

Awtar (5, E2)
Lebanese $$$$
With its opulent Bedouin tent-like atmosphere, mouth-watering meze and live music, Awtar provides a fantastic setting for that big Arabic-style night out. Take the Lebanese lead; arrive late, fill the table

with meze, order some succulent meat dishes and settle in for a long night of band- and belly dance-watching.
☎ 317 2222 ✉ Grand Hyatt Dubai, Al-Qataiyat Rd ✆ 7pm-3am, Sun-Fri

Basta Art Café (2, C2)
Café $
Set in the courtyard of a traditional Bastakia house, this café makes an atmospheric stop on a snoop around the Bastakia Quarter (p9). The food is respectable café fare with a slightly Middle Eastern twist, and the local art is usually worth a perusal.
☎ 353 5071 ✉ Al-Faheidi St, Bastakia ✆ 10am-8pm

Bastakiah Nights (2, C2)
Arabian $$$
With its wonderful setting in a restored house in the Bastakia Quarter, this recently opened restaurant takes full advantage of its location by offering a taste of traditional Arabian food through its set or à la carte menu. There are numerous rooms for private and romantic dining (book ahead) and in the cooler months, open seating

DINING DURING RAMADAN

The holy month of Ramadan sees Muslims fasting from dawn to dusk. As soon as the fast is broken, however, Dubai comes alive with Ramadan tents at just about every hotel with feasting going on long into the early hours of the morning before the fast starts again. Despite the fasting, residents often put on weight during Ramadan! For visitors to Dubai, Ramadan means no eating, drinking or smoking in public during daylight hours. Bars and pubs are shut until 7pm, live music is prohibited and Dubai's dance club turntables spin to a halt. Hotels have rooms set aside for dining or offer room service during the daylight hours. For Ramadan dates, see p84.

is available on the roof. No alcohol.

☎ 353 7772 ✉ Near the Rulers Court, off Al-Faheidi St, Bastakia ⏱ 12.30pm-midnight Sat-Thu, 2pm-midnight Fri

Dôme (2, B3)
Café $$
The action at BurJuman has moved to the flashy new end of the building, but this Aussie café stays busy serving up good coffee, gourmet sandwiches and great cakes. The outside seating is packed in the cooler months. There's a popular branch at Souq Madinat Jumeirah (p39).

☎ 355 6004 ✉ BurJuman Centre, Sheikh Khalifa bin Zayed Rd ⏱ 7.30am-11.30pm

Indochine (right)

Elements Café (5, E2)
Café $$
A stylish shopping stop, the eclectic interior features an even more eclectic menu. Tapas and sushi, Thai soups and tenderloin – they're all together, but quite unexpectedly well done. However, as it's in the shopping mall there's no alcohol served.

☎ 324 4252 ✉ Wafi City, Al-Qataiyat Rd ⏱ 10am-1am Sat-Thu, noon-1am Fri

Il Rustico (3, E2)
Italian $$$
This *molto* popular Italian eatery keeps customers happy with its amiable service and no-nonsense menu. It's a homely little restaurant, but the great pastas, wood-fired pizzas and irresistible home-made bread will keep your focus on what's on the table.

☎ 398 2222 ✉ Rydges Plaza Hotel, Al-Dhiyafah Rd, Satwa Roundabout ⏱ noon-3pm & 6pm-midnight Ⓥ

Indochine (5, E2)
Vietnamese $$$$
The Grand Hyatt's open kitchens reveal a virtual army of chefs working in its bewildering array of dining establishments – most, however, appear to be shoehorned into

Indochine's kitchen. As soon as the fragrant bowl of fresh herbs, rice cakes and peanut dip hits the table you know it's all about freshness. The à la carte menu is fabulous (try the minced duck), while the set menu is excellent for Vietnamese neophytes.

☎ 317 2222 ✉ Grand Hyatt Dubai, Al-Qataiyat Rd ⏱ 7-11.30pm daily, until 1am Wed & Thu

Lemongrass (2, A5)
Thai $$
An independent (no alcohol) favourite of expats, the excellent (and hot!) traditional Thai cuisine keeps the doors swinging and the delivery guys busy. Salads and curries are popular and an order of the Lemongrass set – a selection of starters for two – is almost obligatory.

☎ 334 2325 ✉ near Lamcy Plaza ⏱ noon-midnight Ⓥ

Medzo (5, E2)
Italian $$$
An inventive menu sets modish Medzo apart from the myriad Italian restaurants monopolising Dubai. A wider Mediterranean approach affords Medzo some interesting taste combinations and, while some dishes are a little over-thought or overwrought, there are far more hits than

Bella Donna (p54)

misses. The outdoor seating is lovely in cooler weather.
☎ 324 0000 ✉ Pyramids, Wafi City, Al-Qataiyat Rd
🕑 12.30-3pm & 7.30-11.30pm

Peppercrab (5, E2)
Singaporean $$$$
The busy open kitchen and huge fish tanks are almost a tourist attraction in their own right, but the fresh fish and shellfish are the real draw at this smart restaurant. The signature dish is fantastic, but there are plenty of innovative creations on the menu as well.
☎ 317 2222 ✉ Grand Hyatt Dubai, Al-Qataiyat Rd
🕑 7-11.30pm Mon-Sat, till 1am Wed & Thu

Seville's (5, E2)
Spanish Tapas $$$
The popular outside terrace and excellent sangria are the main draws, but the tapas is good enough to hold its own. Favourites such as *Gambas al Ajillo* (prawns in garlic and oil) and *Chorizo a la Sidra* (Spanish sausage cooked in cider) are standouts.
☎ 324 7300 ✉ Pyramids, Wafi City, Al-Qataiyat Rd

🕑 noon-2am Wed-Sat, noon-3am Thu & Fri

Thai Chi (5, E2)
Contemporary Thai & Chinese $$$
This could be a muddle of pan-Asian plates, but the Thai and Chinese menus are thankfully kept separate at this dual-cuisine restaurant. The Thai staples are well executed and if you're popping over the Great Wall the Peking duck is a must.
☎ 324 4100 ✉ Pyramids, Wafi City, Al-Qataiyat Rd
🕑 noon-3pm & 7.30-midnight

SHEIKH ZAYED RD

Benjarong (3, C3)
Thai $$$$
Refinement is the key word at this elegant Royal Thai restaurant, from the discreet Thai music and dance to the knowledgeable service. However, there's nothing understated about the fantastic flavours with soups such as the *Tom Yam Goong* packing a pungent punch and the mains equally flavourful.
☎ 343 3333 ✉ Dusit Dubai
🕑 7.30pm-midnight

Exchange Grill (3, E3)
Steakhouse $$$$
Arguably the most elegant of Dubai's numerous steakhouses, the ambience is very 'post deal–making dinner'. Modelled on the Oak Room at the Plaza Hotel in New York, the menu features prime cuts of meat and well-chosen vintage wines worthy of the New York institution.
☎ 311 8000 ✉ Fairmont
🕑 7pm-1am

Hoi An (3, C3)
Contemporary Vietnamese $$$$
Just as the ancient city of Hoi An was an East–West trading centre, the wonderful French Vietnamese food on offer at this chic restaurant bridges cultures with ease. The starters are always inventive and mains such as the lemongrass duck breast are a highlight.
☎ 343 8888 ✉ Shangri-La Hotel 🕑 7.30pm-1am **V**

Marrakech
(3, C3)
Moroccan $$$$
Dubai offers up some great Moroccan cuisine these days and Marrakech is a top-tier venue to experience it.

RESTAURANTS THAT MEAN BUSINESS
If you're flying in on business, hit the ground running by suggesting *the* best restaurant for sealing that deal. Here's what your business associates will be telling their head office the next day:
- Exchange Grill (p54) – 'We can do business'
- Tagine (p57) – 'I think we were being seduced'
- Trader Vic's (p54) – 'We might have signed a contract last night, but I can't remember…'
- Verre (p50) – 'These guys are very smooth operators'
- Vu's (p54) – 'Now that's an expense account!'

Lime Tree Café (opposite)

It does the Moroccan classics well – try the couscous royale, chicken *tagen* (casserole) or the lamb shanks – and savour the live music as well. Book a table by the fountain or a romantic booth.
☎ 343 8888 ✉ Shangri-La Hotel ⏰ 1-3pm & 8pm-midnight

Noodle House (3, D3)
Asian $$
Noodle House has been packing in punters hungry for its selection of pan-Asian staples since it opened. This sort of popularity usually translates to a waiting list (no bookings), so if it's packed put your name down and head to Agency (p59) for a tipple. There's another branch at Madinat Souq, but we prefer the food here.

☎ 319 8757 ✉ Emirates Towers ⏰ noon-11.30pm

Spectrum on One (3, E3)
Modern Global $$$
While the concept of having eight open kitchens serving up cuisine from around the globe sounds more food court than five-star, Spectrum on One manages to sate disparate tastes quite well. Still, it seems a little odd when one diner's gobbling down fresh oysters while a companion sips a green curry, but if it manages to stop the age-old holiday-troubling 'what will we eat?' argument, it's working.
☎ 311 8101 ✉ Fairmont ⏰ 7pm-1am

Trader Vic's (3, D3)
Polynesian $$$$
While this branch of the long-standing Polynesian-themed chain is long overdue for a makeover, the lethal cocktails (try the signature Mai Tai) and alcohol-soaking starters keep this Dubai mainstay busy. Try something cooked in the Chinese wood-fired clay oven for a main course. There's another branch at Souq Madinat Jumeirah (p39).
☎ 331 1111 ✉ Crowne Plaza Hotel ⏰ 12.30-3pm & 7.30-11.30pm

Vu's (3, D3)
Fine Dining $$$$
This restaurant atop Emirates Towers has the wow factor in spades – a chic interior, spectacular views and an impressive menu with a mix of French and Italian cuisine. While it's been a bit of a high stakes gamble in the past (unless dining is on someone else's expense account), it's thankfully become one of Dubai's more consistent fine dining experiences.
☎ 319 8771 ✉ Emirates Towers ⏰ 12.30-3pm & 7.30pm-midnight

JUMEIRAH

Bella Donna (3, B2)
Italian $$
While malls and good food rarely share the same address, the pasta and pizzas at this stylish eatery are fresh and tasty. The coffee is also noteworthy, making it a fine place to refuel during an extended shopping expedition. Balcony tables are popular during the cooler months.
☎ 344 7710 ✉ Mercato, Jumeirah Rd ⏰ 11am-11pm

BiCE (4, A1)
Italian $$$$
Considered by many to be the best Italian in town, this understated, elegant restaurant uses quality imported ingredients and treats them with respect – all too rare a combination in Dubai. Excellent breads, a well-selected wine list and well-drilled staff help cement its reputation.
☎ 399 1111 ✉ Hilton Dubai Jumeirah, Al-Sufouh Rd, Al-Mina al-Seyahi ⏰ noon-3pm & 7pm-midnight

TOP FIVE HOTEL RESTAURANTS
- Verre (p50) – at the Hilton Dubai Creek (p70)
- Indochine (p52) – at the Grand Hyatt Dubai (p70)
- Tagine (p57) – at the One&Only Royal Mirage (p68)
- Blue Elephant (p49) – at Al-Bustan Rotana Hotel (p69)
- Zheng He's (p57) – at Al-Qasr (p69)

Chandelier (4, A1)
Lebanese $$$
After getting the gastronomic nod from the discerning Lebanese expat community, Chandelier has become the hit of the new Marina Walk. In the cooler months it resembles a downtown Beirut restaurant, with outdoor tables filled with groups enjoying the excellent meze and smoking *sheesha*. We can only imagine how much arak will go down once it get its long-promised alcohol licence.
☎ 366 3606 ✉ Marina Walk, Dubai Marina, Al-Sufouh Rd, Al-Mina al-Seyahi ⏱ 8.30am-3.30pm & 6.30pm-2.30am

Eauzone (4, A1)
Fine Dining $$$$
A romantic evening with adventurous food awaits those making their way across the low-lit boardwalk to the tranquil pool-surrounded setting of this alluring restaurant. The contemporary menu takes some Asian-inspired diversions and it's only the occasional hiccup in service that threatens to spoil the magic of the inventive fare on offer.
☎ 399 9999 ✉ One&Only Royal Mirage, Al-Mina al-Seyahi ⏱ noon-3.30pm & 7.30pm-11.30pm

Japengo Café (3, D1)
Café $$
Perpetually packed, especially in the cooler months, when you take a seat at Japengo you'd be forgiven for thinking that the food was arriving at tables from several different restaurants. While pizza and sushi should never share ink on the same menu, this being Dubai we're just glad they're not sharing the same plate.
☎ 345 4979 ✉ Palm Strip Shopping Mall, opposite Jumeirah Mosque, Jumeirah Rd ⏱ noon-midnight

La Baie (4, A1)
Fine Dining $$$$
The formal atmosphere of the Ritz-Carlton's signature restaurant feels a little transplanted in Dubai – it's decidedly *not* typical beach resort dining. However, if you're craving refined comfort food coupled with exemplary service and a first-rate wine list, you can always pretend it's not bikini weather outside.
☎ 399 4000 ✉ Ritz-Carlton Hotel, Al-Sufouh Rd, Al-Mina al-Seyahi ⏱ 7-11pm, closed Sun

Lime Tree Café (3, D1)
Café $
This pleasant green villa has been keeping homesick Western expats sane for years. The daily menu features a range of Western café staples such as frittatas, quiches and salads along with the kind of funky atmosphere that provides comfort for those homesick blues.
☎ 349 8498 ✉ Near Jumeirah Mosque, Jumeirah Rd ⏱ 7.30am-8pm

Majlis Al Bahar (4, D1)
Mediterranean $$$$
While the Burj Al Arab's signature restaurant, Al-Mahara, requires you to take a phoney 'submarine' ride and stare at a fish tank all night, Majlis Al Bahar offers a stunning vista of the iconic Burj through the palm trees of its beachside location. The light Mediterranean menu may feature salads and soups of a quality that can be found elsewhere, but none can match the view. Forget your manners and

It's fresh and tasty at Bella Donna (opposite)

ORIENTALIST'S DELIGHT

For those whom the idea of the Middle East is filled with the Oriental paintings of Jean-Léon Gérôme or the storytelling of Scheherazade in *The Thousand and One Nights,* who are we to dispel your Orientalist notions? Here are some restaurants that fully live up to those Orientalist fantasies:

• Awtar (p51) – ultra-refined version of the Lebanese 'big night out'
• Bastakiah Nights (p51) – dine like the 20th century never happened in this restored Bastakia house
• Shahrzad (p50) – old Persia bottled and brought to Dubai
• Tagine (opposite) – Moroccan ambience right down to the fez-wearing waiters

grab the seat with the best sightlines.
☎ 301 7000 ✉ beach end of Burj Al Arab, Jumeirah Rd, Umm Suqeim ⏱ 7pm-midnight

Maria Bonita's Taco Shop
(4, E1)
Mexican $$
A welcoming little slice of Mexico (very Vera Cruz) down Jumeirah way, this laid-back restaurant offers up tasty authentic dishes right down to the tortilla soup and *queso fundido* (cheese fondue). Beats all the 'Tex-Mex' non-sense on offer in Dubai hands down, but before you hit the waiter with an order for *dos*

cerveza (two beers) remind yourself that it's unlicensed.
☎ 395 5576 ✉ Umm al-Sheif St, Umm Suqeim ⏱ 7.30am-8pm

Marina Seafood Market
(4, D1)
Seafood $$$$
At the end of the breakwater at this landmark hotel is a breathtaking view of Dubai's iconic Burj Al Arab. The fresh local and imported seafood is as much a feast for the eyes as the Burj itself. Perfect for a leisurely Sauvignon Blanc–fuelled seafood lunch.
☎ 406 8181 ✉ Jumeirah Beach Hotel, Jumeirah Rd ⏱ 12.30-4pm & 7pm-2am

Mezzanine (4, A1)
Fine Dining $$$$
The inaugural venture of Gary Robinson, former head chef to Prince Charles, is the first genuine Dubai challenger to peerless Verre (p50). The subtly imaginative 'British Modern' cuisine reveals a chef with wonderful technique; the white-on-white décor with eccentric touches such as chandeliers and silver faux-antique sideboards in clear glass cases creates a whimsical atmosphere. Book well ahead.
☎ 399 8888 ✉ Le Meridien Grosvenor House, West Marina Beach ⏱ 7pm-midnight

Nina (4, A1)
Contemporary Indian $$$
Along with Asha's (p51), Nina sets the bar high for contemporary Indian in Dubai. If you find the seductive orange and purple interior too mesmerising to concentrate on the menu, just order the tasting selection, soak up the sumptuous atmosphere and await the equally delicious fare.
☎ 399 9999 ✉ Arabian Court, One&Only Royal Mirage, Al-Sufouh Rd, Al-Mina al-Seyahi ⏱ 12.30-4pm & 7pm-2am

Pierchic (4, C1)
Seafood $$$$
The stroll down the pier to this water-bound restaurant is best taken for dinner, when Madinat Jumeirah twinkles onshore and the Burj Al Arab lightshow is mesmerising. Perhaps too aware of the competition offered by the stunning vistas, Pierchic's menu tries too hard, with

some dish descriptions reading more like shopping lists than individual dishes. If you like your seafood simply presented and flavoured, order the fresh seafood platter, sit back and soak up the view.
☎ 399 9999 ✉ Al-Qasr, Madinat Jumeirah, Al-Sufouh Rd 🕒 noon-3pm & 7-11.30pm

Prime Rib (4, A1)
Steakhouse $$$$
This is the king of the beach resort (m)eateries, with its smart neo-deco interior, informed service and gentle jazz soundtrack. While someone will inevitably order seafood (and it's fine), most people arrive with one thing in mind — American Angus beef. It's perfectly cooked to order, simply served and deserves something special from the excellent wine list.
☎ 399 5555 ✉ Le Royal Meridien, Al-Sufouh Rd, Al-Mina al-Seyahi 🕒 7pm-midnight

Retro (4, A1)
Modern European $$$$
Retro serves up adventurous contemporary cuisine that, while not up to Verre's (p50) exacting standards, excites with some well-executed dishes. In the cooler months you can escape the retro-futuristic décor and dine out on the terrace.
☎ 399 3333 ✉ Le Meridien, Al-Sufouh Rd, Al-Mina al-Seyahi 🕒 7-11pm

Shoo Fee Ma Fee (4, C1)
Moroccan $$$
Literally meaning 'what's up?', Shoo Fee Ma Fee offers up three floors of Moroccan ambience overlooking the appealing waterways of the souq. The pigeon pastilla and other favourites offer flavour melodies as true as the authentic in-house band, but the more inventive dishes on the menu don't always hit the right notes.
☎ 366 8888 ✉ Souq Madinat Jumeirah, Al-Sufouh Rd 🕒 7-11.30pm, drinks until 12.30am

Tagine (4, A1)
Moroccan $$$$
Despite increasingly stiff competition such as Shoo Fee Ma Fee, Tagine still arguably serves up the best Moroccan vibe in Dubai. The classics such as harira soup and pigeon pastilla make authentically pleasing starters and the tagine and couscous dishes transport your taste buds directly to Fez.
☎ 399 9999 ✉ One&Only Royal Mirage, Al-Sufouh Rd, Al-Mina al-Seyahi 🕒 7-11pm

Zheng He's (4, C1)
Contemporary Chinese $$$$
From the authentic dim sum to the inventive desserts, Zheng He's serves up wonderful flavours (try any seafood dish on offer) with eye-catching presentations. While the interior is dazzling, book well ahead for an alfresco table with a stunning view of the Burj Al Arab.
☎ 366 8888 ✉ Mina A' Salam, Madinat Jumeirah, Al-Sufouh Rd 🕒 noon-3pm & 7-11.30pm

SIMPLY SHWARMA
As the sun goes down in Dubai the *shwarma* stands open up, offering the Middle East's version of fast food long into the night. Here are some of the best places in Dubai; don't forget to order a fresh juice to go with it.
• Ashwaq Cafeteria (2, D2; cnr Al-Soor & Sikkat al-Khail Sts, Bur Dubai) — Perfectly placed for a post–souq shopping snack
• Automatic (2, B3; off Khalid bin al-Waleed Rd) — OK, so it's more restaurant than *shwarma* stand, but Automatic is the elder statesperson of Dubai's Lebanese scene, with branches all around the city
• Beirut (3, E2; Al-Dhiyafah St, Satwa) — The Al-Dhiyafah strips' most popular *shwarma*
• Saj Express (3, C3; Sheikh Zayed Rd) — Simply the best *shwarma* on Sheikh Zayed Rd

Entertainment

Dubai is a cosmopolitan city, and its bars and clubs are as hip and stylish as they come, fusing exotic Oriental and contemporary Western styles in their design and music.

To meet the needs of the population, an increasing number of international DJs are racking up frequent flyer miles coming to Dubai. There are DJ nights every day of the week, frequent one-off events, and all types of music – R&B, jazz, soul, funk, trip-hop, tribal, house, electronica, Arabic, African, Latino, Euro-pop and an increasing fusion of styles.

With endless options for drinking and dancing, the nights can be long. They won't end at dawn, because most clubs close at 3am, but they'll probably start early with a sunset drink at a waterside bar. Licensing laws require venues serving alcohol to be attached to hotels or private clubs and as a result a big night out can come with a hefty bill.

Dubai weekends are also long, lasting from Wednesday to Saturday nights. Thursday and Friday are holidays for the government sector, whereas those working in the private sector have Friday and Saturday off. This means visitors to Dubai get to have twice as much fun, another multicultural advantage.

A night out at Grand Cineplex (p63)

Monthly magazines *What's On* and *Time Out* have listings, or pick up free guides and leaflets promoting clubs, dance parties and gigs from cafés or bars; information is also available at Virgin Megastore (p45) and Ohm Records (p45). Look for club guides **Mumtazz** (www.mumtazz.com), **Fever** (ihavefever@fluidproduction.com) and **Infusion** (www.infusion.ae) and check out www.9714.com and www.globalfunkdxb.com.

For tickets to concerts and major events at Dubai Media City, the Tennis Stadium and Madinat Jumeirah, from Destiny's Child to Pavarotti, phone the Time Out ticketline on 800 4669, buy online at www.itptickets.com or www.boxofficeme.com, or email marketing@motivate.com. For info about Dubai Tennis Stadium acts, visit www.aviationclubonline.com.

ITINERARY: SUNSET OVER JUMEIRAH

It's hard to beat a sunset drink on the veranda at **Bahri Bar** (opposite) to set the mood for romance. While the sky's still glowing orange, take a stroll around the waterside wooden decks of Madinat Jumeirah to **Ushna** (p61) for a quiet predinner drink. Walk along the wooden wharf for dinner on the water at **Pierchic** (p56, make sure you book a table overlooking the magical Al-Qasr and Burj Al Arab). Cab it to **Rooftop** (p60) for a nightcap under the stars, finishing the evening with a moonlit walk around the hotel's gorgeous gardens.

SPECIAL EVENTS

January–February *Dubai Marathon* (www.dubaimarathon.org) – A full marathon as well as a 10km run and a 3km 'fun run'.

Dubai Shopping Festival (www.mydsf.com) – A month of fireworks, frenzied shopping, full hotels and traffic jams, from mid-January.

Dubai International Jazz Festival – Held during the Shopping Festival, the event is staged at Dubai Media City over three nights.

Dubai Fashion Week – Two weeks after launching Spring/Summer haute couture collections in Paris, the fashion houses head to Dubai for five days.

Dubai Tennis Championships (www.dubaitennischampionships.com) – Women's and men's events are held over two weeks from late February.

March *Dubai Desert Classic* (www.dubaidesertclassic.com) – The Dubai Desert Classic lures some of the best golfers in the world by offering one of the largest purses on the golfing calendar.

Dubai World Cup (www.dubaiworldcup.com) – The Dubai International Racing Carnival, which runs from February through to the end of March, culminates in the Dubai World Cup, the world's richest horse race.

April *Sharjah International Biennial* (www.sharjahbiennial.org) – Held biennially during April, May and June, this provocative expo is increasingly attracting global attention, especially for its Middle Eastern and Emirati art.

June *Dubai Summer Surprises* (www.mydsf.com) – The summer version of the Dubai Shopping Festival, the surprise is the furnace that greets you outside the arrivals hall.

December *Dubai International Film Festival* (www.dubaifilmfest.com) – The clumsy organisation and emphasis on imported stars failed to detract from the excellent Arabic film programme on offer at the inaugural festival in 2004.

Dubai Rugby 7s (www.dubairugby7s.com) – One of Dubai's most social sporting events, it's the highlight of many expatriates' year.

BARS & PUBS

Agency (3, D3)
An extensive wine list, excellent wines by the glass, themed tasting selections, and delicious tapas-sized snacks used to keep this stylish city bar busy. A favourite after-work spot, a good late-nighter, it had no match. Until…another opened at Souq Madinat Jumeirah (4, C1).
☎ 330 0000 ✉ Emirates Towers Shopping Blvd, Sheikh Zayed Rd ⏱ noon-1am Sat-Thu, 3pm-1am Fri

Bahri Bar (4, C1)
Recline on the rattan lounges on the vast veranda of this colonial Arabian bar (slip your shoes off if you dare), sip a chilled white, enjoy the sea breeze and take in the breathtaking views – sunset one side, Burj Al Arab on the other. You'll feel like you're on holiday, even if you're not.
☎ 366 8888 ✉ Mina A' Salam, Madinat Jumeirah, Al-Sufouh Rd, Jumeirah ⏱ noon-2am

Barasti Bar (4, A1)
While the weekend beach parties are popular with a tanned young crowd, this laidback outdoor seaside bar is also a perfect place to watch the sun go down with a drink on a balmy afternoon.
☎ 399 3333 ✉ Le Meridien Mina Seyahi Resort, Al-Sufouh Rd, Jumeirah ⏱ 6pm-2am

BarZar (4, C1)

The weekends are big at BarZar, when there are cheap (and sometimes free) drinks. The sleek bar tends to be quiet upstairs, from where you can look on to the raucous downstairs bar where there's usually sport on TV. Outside, you can chill out in beanbags by the water.

☎ 366 6348 ✉ Souq Madinat Jumeirah, Al-Sufouh Rd, Jumeirah ⏱ noon-1am

Buddha Bar (4, A1)

Just like its sister Paris bar – only more Shanghai than Thai – a big Buddha presides over this exotic space. Red chandeliers, hanging glass beads, the waitresses' red Manchu coats and a warren of rooms create a mood of drama and intrigue. The place also features Oriental chill-out music, delicious cocktails and a buzzy vibe – book ahead so you don't miss out!

☎ 399 8888 ✉ Le Meridien Grosvenor House, West Marina Beach, Jumeirah ⏱ noon-2am, to 3am Thu & Fri

Ginseng (5, E2)

This funky Far Eastern bar with Chinese murals and mirrors on its walls serves up the best *caiparinhas* (sugarcane liquor and lime cocktail) in the city and some excellent drink deals, including cocktails for Dh19 from 7pm to 9pm daily during Ginseng Hour. You can soak it all up with some excellent spicy Asian tapas.

☎ 324 8200 ✉ Wafi Pyramids, Wafi City, Oud Metha

Rd, Bur Dubai ⏱ 7pm-2am Fri-Wed, 7pm-3am Thu

Irish Village (5, E2)

The beer garden at this Irish pub is popular with expats, and the after-work crowd packs the place out on Wednesday nights. On weekends it's a lovely spot to laze on the grass by the 'lake' with the ducks and a Guinness. There's a good selection of draught beers and live music.

☎ 282 4750 ✉ Aviation Club, Dubai Tennis Stadium, Al-Garhoud Rd, Deira ⏱ 11am-1.30am

Ku Bu (2, D3)

Kick back with some cocktails and cool music in this dark, funky DJ bar with contemporary Afro-cool interior and secluded spots made more so by plush drapes.

☎ 205 7033 ✉ InterContinental Dubai Hotel, Baniyas Rd, Deira ⏱ 7pm-3am

LeftBank (4, C1)

The very stylish décor glows at night and, while it's calm enough for a decent conversation during the week, the place pumps on weekend nights with groups of expats letting their hair down.

☎ 368 6171 ✉ Souq Madinat Jumeirah, Al-Sufouh Rd, Jumeirah ⏱ noon-2am

Lotus One (3, E3)

As you sip a lychee-and-ginger martini, the DJ spins lounge sounds, the colours of the fibre-optic lighting subtly swing the mood from chill out to groove and you'll think to yourself: Dubai has arrived.

☎ 329 3200 ✉ World Trade Centre, off Sheikh Zayed Rd ⏱ noon-2am

Rooftop (4, A1)

Expectations formed as you climb the candle-lit stairs are met the moment you arrive on the Rooftop – Persian carpets, banquettes and Moroccan lanterns – it's everyone's *Arabian Nights'* fantasy. Once you settle in with a drink and the sun sets you won't want to wake from this dream. Groups should book the corner seating area for the full effect.

☎ 399 9999 ✉ One&Only Royal Mirage, Al-Sufouh Rd, Jumeirah ⏱ 5pm-12.45am

Sho Cho (3, E1)

During the hot summer months chill out to the DJ's vibes from the funky leather

Head to Wafi City for Ginseng Hour (left)

SOLO TRAVELLERS
Good places for…
- reading a book with a Chardonnay on a sunny afternoon – Bahri Bar (p59)
- drinking with friendly Guinness-guzzling expats – Irish Village (opposite)
- chatting up Champagne-swilling singles – Agency (p59)
- meeting hospitable Scotch-hugging Gulf men – Vu's Bar (below)

sofas in this groovy sushi bar. In winter the DJ moves outside to the wooden beachside deck so Dubai's hipsters can take in the balmy breeze, deep house and tribal beats, and each other.
☎ 346 1111 ✉ Dubai Marine Beach Resort & Spa, Jumeirah Rd, Jumeirah ⏰ 7.30pm-12.30am Sat-Wed, 7.30pm-2.30am Thu & Fri

Skyview Bar (4, D1)
Cocktail bar of the world's first seven-star hotel it may be, however, a window seat's required to divert your attention from the crass décor to the dizzying coastal views. The Dh175 (per person) paid at the security gate can be redeemed at the bar; the hors d'oeuvres are delicious.
☎ 301 7777 ✉ Burj Al Arab, Jumeirah Rd ⏰ 11am-2am; phone ahead, booking with credit card required

Ushna (4, C1)
The Indian fusion restaurant may be glam (fuchsia interior, hanging seats and chandeliers) but the funky candle-lit bar outside is fantastic. Settle into a lounge, listen to some chilled vibes, and savour the Madinat Jumeirah views and buzzy crowd below on weekends.
☎ 368 6506 ✉ Souq Madinat Jumeirah, Al-Sufouh Rd, Jumeirah ⏰ 12.30pm-2am

Vintage (5, E2)
While aficionados love the extensive wine list, it's the wide range of grape by the glass and delicious cheese plates that keep the regulars coming back. Makes a great predinner meeting spot.
☎ 324 0000 ✉ Wafi Pyramids, Wafi City, Oud Metha, Bur Dubai ⏰ 6pm-1.30am

Vu's Bar (3, D3)
The stupendous views of Dubai from 220m is what draws the tourists up the glass elevator, but residents come for the decent wines by the glass, stylish setting and friendly atmosphere.
☎ 330 0000 ✉ 51st fl, Emirates Towers, Sheikh Zayed Rd ⏰ 6pm-2am

CLUBS

Boudoir (3, E1)
Red velvet booths, hanging glass beads and crystal chandeliers make baroque Boudoir the glammest bar in town. Starting the night in style as a restaurant-cum–cocktail bar, as soon as the clock strikes 12 it becomes a decadent dance club. Free champagne for girls on Tuesdays and Fridays.
☎ 345 5995 ✉ Dubai Marine Beach Resort, Jumeirah Rd ⏰ 7.30pm-3am

Chameleon & Vice (5, E2)
Ubercool Chameleon offers cocktails and dinner with

live jazz or world music, and dancing later. The DJ spins funky grooves and uplifting house on weekends; midweek it's Arabesque, Parisian fusion and Afro-Latino. Vice is a vodka-and-champagne bar offering the most extensive range of both in the region.
☎ 324 0000 ✉ Wafi Pyramids, Wafi City, Oud Metha, Bur Dubai ⏰ Tue-Sun 7pm-3am

iBO (5, E2)
A few months after the hot club Terminal was terminated, its black walls were whitewashed, disco ball and velvet sofas installed, shagpile rugs scattered across the concrete floors and iBO was born. From the same crew you now get midweek events, from movie nights to jazz – and the most interesting DJs from around the globe flying in on weekends.
☎ 398 2206 ✉ Millennium Airport Hotel, Al-Garhoud Rd, Deira ⏰ 8pm-3am

Kasbar (4, A1)
This glamorous Moroccan-themed nightclub gives you the chance to dance to Arabic pop and fusion, and possibly meet a wealthy young sheikh.
☎ 399 9999 ✉ One&Only Royal Mirage, Al-Sufouh Rd, Jumeirah ⏰ 9.30pm-3am Mon-Sat

MIX (5, E2)
Dubai's first 'superclub', MIX pulls a crowd for its people-watching opportunities from the bar, its bongo players and podium dancers, international DJ events (the best nights by far), and swish VIP area.
☎ 317 2570 ✉ Grand Hyatt Dubai, Al-Qataiyat Rd, Bur Dubai ☾ 9pm-3am, closed Sat

Oxygen (5, E2)
The baroque interior, DJs and drink promotions keep the locals coming, despite the tiny dance floor. A good weekend choice this side of the Creek, regardless of which DJ is spinning the soul, R&B, Arabic, house or just plain pop.
☎ 282 0000 ✉ Al-Bustan Rotana, Casablanca Rd, Deira ☾ 6pm-3am

Tangerine (3, E3)
Head here early if you want to check out the rich Oriental interior over a drink – due to the DJs and drinks promotions, this club hots up after 11pm. Dress up – when the place is packed the power-crazed door staff can be very selective.
☎ 332 5555 ✉ Fairmont, Sheikh Zayed Rd ☾ 8pm-3am

Trilogy (4, C1)
Another drinking, dining and dance spot, the super-stylish Trilogy has bars over several levels to cater for different tastes. Busy most nights, it's packed on weekends when it's best for people-watching. Book your tickets if an international DJ is on.
☎ 366 6917 ✉ Souq Madinat Jumeirah, Al-Sufouh Rd, Jumeirah ☾ 9pm-3am

Zinc (3, D3)
Although Zinc suffers a bit of an identity crisis, it's popular with expats and tourists who take over its dance floor early in the night (compared to most Dubai clubs). Although the music is fairly unadventurous (and the live music a dance-floor clearer) it can be lots of fun.
☎ 331 1111 ✉ Crowne Plaza Hotel, Sheikh Zayed Rd ☾ 7pm-3am

SHEESHA CAFÉS

Cosmo Café (3, D3)
Very popular with stylish young Arabs, this casual café is the place to head for some beautiful people–

watching with your apple *sheesha*.
☎ 332 6569 ✉ Tower, Sheikh Zayed Rd ☾ 8.30-1am

Kanzaman (2, C1)
As much a restaurant as it is a *sheesha* joint, the waterside location, sprawling size and good food at Kanzaman make it very popular with Emiratis and Arab families, who have *sheesha* with their meals.
☎ 393 9914 ✉ Heritage & Diving Village, Shindagha, Bur Dubai ☾ 11am-3am

Shisha Courtyard (4, A1)
One of the most atmospheric places in Dubai to smoke *sheesha:* recline on cushions in the Moroccan-style *majlis* (meeting room) of the Arabian courtyard and choose from more than 20 flavours.
☎ 399 9999 ✉ One&Only Royal Mirage, Jumeirah ☾ 7pm-1am

Souq Madinat Jumeirah Central Plaza (4, C1)
The souq location, live oud player, long list of flavours, and cool breezes on a winter evening make this one of the nicest spots to have *sheesha*.
☎ 366 8888 ✉ Souq Madinat Jumeirah, Al-Sufouh Rd, Jumeirah ☾ 10am-11pm

CINEMAS

Century Cinemas (3, B1)
It shows the same Hollywood hits as the other theatres, but this cinema complex has an arty bent, hosting films from the Dubai International Film Festival, and the odd embassy-organised film week.
☎ 349 8765 ✉ Mercato Mall, Jumeirah Rd 💲 Dh30

ITINERARY: CLUBBING IT IN DUBAI
Start a city-based night of clubbing with cocktails at **Ginseng** (p60) then head next door for vodkas at **Vice** (p61) before hitting the dance floor at **Chameleon**. Take a taxi to **Sho Cho** (p60) to cool down on its beachside deck before heading inside to do your thing at decadent **Boudoir** (p61). Still up for some action? Depending on where you're sleeping, you could head down the beach to **Trilogy** (right), into the city to **iBO** (p61) or finish at **Tangerine** (above). You probably won't be going anywhere the next day!

Bawdy Bollywood at Lamcy Cinema (below)

CineStar (2, D6)
Catch the latest Hollywood blockbusters, American indie flicks and the occasional British and European film at this popular state-of-the-art 11-screen complex.
☎ 294 9000 ✉ Deira City Centre, Deira 💲 Dh20 before 6pm, Dh30 after 6pm

Grand Cineplex (5, E2)
At this hi-tech 10-screen complex showing the latest English-language movies, you'll also find a good array of cafés, DVDs, music, fashion and a bank to cash up after spending all your dirhams!
☎ 324 2000 ✉ Grand Hyatt Dubai, next to Wafi City, Bur Dubai 💲 Dh25-30

Lamcy Cinema (2, A6)
In contrast to most of the run-down cinemas showing Hindi, Malayalam and Tamil films, this two-screen cinema screening predominantly Bollywood movies is modern and comfortable.
☎ 336 8808 ✉ Lamcy Plaza, Al-Qataiyat Rd, Karama, Bur Dubai 💲 Dh20

Movies Under the Stars (5, E2)
On Sunday nights during the cooler autumn, winter and spring months, you can sink into a beanbag and plunge your hands into some big boxes of popcorn for themed outdoor film nights.
☎ 324 0000 ✉ Wafi City Rooftop, Wafi Mall, Bur Dubai 💲 8pm-late 💲 free

LIVE MUSIC

Opportunities to see jazz and classical music are gradually increasing in Dubai, but it's still rare to see good alternative or original music and international music that isn't mainstream. International acts tour infrequently; most perform at the Dubai Media City Amphitheatre and Dubai Tennis Stadium.

Blue Bar (3, D3)
The blue glass, dark wood and minimalist look of this bar is spoilt by the incessant TV and the somewhat disinterested-looking patrons. If excellent Belgian beers and live jazz and blues keep you happy, you won't mind one bit.
☎ 332 0000 ✉ Novotel, off Sheikh Zayed Rd, behind the Convention Centre 💲 noon-1am

JamBase (4, C1)
This stylish venue packs punters in for live jazz, R&B and soul as well as Deep South cuisine. The bands know how to work a crowd and the dance floor jumps on weekends.
☎ 366 6914 ✉ Souq Madinat Jumeirah, Al-Sufouh Rd, Jumeirah 💲 noon-1am

Jazz on the Green (5, E2)
On Saturday nights during the cooler months you can enjoy live jazz, decent food and excellent wine, on the Cellar's waterside terrace.
☎ 282 9333 ✉ Cellar, Aviation Club, Al-Garhoud, Deira 💲 8pm-2am Sat

Jules (5, E2)
A resident Filipino band performs at this American bar

but the people-watching can prove distracting. Jules attracts a mixed crowd, Filipino expats, Gulf Arabs and single girls from the former Soviet Union – not all here for the music. For those who work up an appetite there's Tex-Mex, Cajun and Filipino food.
☎ 282 4040 ✉ Le Meridien Dubai Hotel, Al-Garhoud, Deira ⏱ 11am-3am

Peanut Butter Jam (5, E2)
During the cooler months (call to check) you can settle in to a beanbag, pick from the barbeque buffet, watch resident guest bands play live acoustic sets, and even join them for a jam session.
☎ 324 4100 ✉ Wafi City, Bur Dubai ⏱ 4-7pm Fri, except summer

Rock Bottom Café (2, B3)
This pick-up joint is a Dubai institution; its reputation is

built on its Bullfrog cocktails (free for the ladies on Sunday nights) and resident rock and cover bands. Saying you ended the night at the Rock Bottom Café means you probably drank more than you should.
☎ 396 3888 ✉ Regent Palace Hotel, Sheikh Khalifa bin Zayed Rd, Bur Dubai ⏱ noon-3am

THEATRE & COMEDY

Laughter Factory (3, D3)
Claiming to be Dubai's premier comedy club (to be fair, at time of writing there were only two) these stand-ups from London's Comedy Store let off steam monthly at Zinc bar at the Crowne Plaza Hotel and Jimmy Dix at the Mövenpick Hotel.
☎ 331 1111, 336 8800, 800 4669 ✉ Zinc, Crowne Plaza Hotel, Sheikh Zayed Rd &

Jimmy Dix, Mövenpick Hotel, 19 St, Oud Metha, Bur Dubai ⏱ 9pm-1am 💲 Dh95

Laughter House (5, E2)
An offshoot of Liverpool's Laughter House, this popular monthly comedy night generally features four of their stand-ups who fly in to town for the night.
☎ 282 4122 ✉ Rainbow Room, Aviation Club ⏱ doors open 7.30pm, show starts 9pm, 1st Tue every month 💲 show Dh70, incl preshow dinner & wine Dh180

Madinat Theatre (4, C2)
The opening of the city's first theatre venue was applauded by Dubai's culture-starved residents. A regular programme of crowd-pleasing entertainment has included Pavarotti, the Russian State Ballet, a French production of Le Petit Prince, a Broadway musical, a Noel Coward play, a Japanese New Age pianist, an Irish folk singer and a Cuban 'dance spectacular' – eclectic to say the least! Performances take place in the Theatre, Arena or outdoors at the enchanting waterside Amphitheatre.
☎ 366 6546, 366 6550 ✉ Souq Madinat Jumeirah, Al-Sufouh Rd, Jumeirah ⏱ box office 10am-11pm, show times vary 💲 Dh60-200

ITINERARY: (MULTI-)CULTURAL IMMERSION
Despite being an Arab city, Dubai's position and international population have made it a multicultural one. Begin a day of immersion in this cosmopolitan culture with a typical Emirati pastime, **camel racing** (opposite). After brunch, catch a Bollywood movie at **Lamcy Cinema** (p63). Enjoy a sunset *sheesha* on the creek and bite to eat at **Kanzaman** (p62) before catching an Emirati football match at a local stadium. Head to **Cosmo** (p62) for *sheesha* and snacks with the beautiful Lebanese people. End the night on the dance floor with the Filipino expats at **Jules** (p63).

DUBAI'S STRAIGHT SHOOTER

This being Dubai, where success is an expectation that is rarely unfulfilled, it comes as no surprise that the UAE's first Olympic medal was gold in colour. Sheikh Ahmed al-Maktoum, a member of Dubai's ruling family, won the men's double trap shoot in style at the 2004 Athens Olympics with an Olympic record–equalling display of cool-headed marksmanship.

SPORT

Camel Racing

Racing of the much beloved camel takes place on Thursday and Friday mornings and on public holidays in winter and spring. Camel racing is a major spectator sport in the UAE, with races starting around 7am and continuing until about 9am. If you're not in Dubai on a racing day, you can usually catch training sessions each morning at about the same time or at around 5.30pm.

Cricket

International cricket is held in nearby Sharjah, with matches held in October, November, March and April; the Sharjah Cup is held in March or April. Participating teams change every year, but one is always India or Pakistan, which attracts the fiercely loyal nationals of both countries. These are usually 'day-night' matches, starting at 2.30pm and finishing under lights at around 10.15pm.

Horse Racing

A love of horses runs deep in Arab blood and over the past few years the racing season in Dubai has gained world attention as has Crown Prince Sheikh Mohammed's Godolphin stables (p30). The Dubai International Racing Carnival runs from February through to the end of March culminating in the **Dubai World Cup** (www.dubaiworldcup.com), the world's richest horse race. Gambling isn't permitted, but the World Cup offers a fantastic people- and silly hat–watching experience. Check the website of the **Emirates Racing Association** (www.emiratesracing.com) for the exact dates of race meetings throughout the year.

Golf

It's not surprising that the **Dubai Desert Classic** (www.dubaidesertclassic .com) attracts some of the best golfers in the world. It's one of the world's richest tournaments, with prize money of US$2.2 million in 2005. Held at the Emirates Golf Club, the tournament runs for four days and takes place in late February or March. Many of Dubai's golf-crazy expats take the whole week off for the opportunity to watch the world's best go round their local course.

Emirates Golf club (p26)

Football

The UAE football (soccer) premiership runs during winter and it's definitely worth attending a match if you're a bit of a football fanatic. Al-Ain has been the most consistent team in recent years and the matches are as worth watching for the electrifying performances of the colour-coordinated cheer squad of drummers and singers as for the on-pitch heroes. Stadiums are dotted around the city. See *Gulf News* for upcoming fixtures.

Tennis

The Dubai Tennis Championships, held over two weeks from late February consists of a Women's Tennis Association event followed by an Association of Tennis Professionals event. There's usually a good turnout of top names for the women's event, and the men's event is finally attracting the big names, too.

Rugby

The Dubai Rugby 7s tournament (www.dubairugby7s.com) takes place at the Dubai Exiles rugby ground and sees many of Dubai's expats worshipping the sport of outdoor beer-drinking. There's also a rugby competition that attracts teams from powerhouses such as New Zealand, France, South Africa and Fiji. It's a popular social event that usually falls in the first weekend of December, attracting around 20,000 enthusiastic spectators for the final.

MAJOR SPORTING VENUES
Dubai Camel Racecourse (5, D2; ☎ 338 2324; off Oud Metha Rd near Nad al-Sheba Club)
Dubai Exiles Rugby Club (5, D3; ☎ 333 1198; www.dubaiexiles.com; Ras al-Khor Rd, near the Dubai Country Club)
Dubai Tennis Stadium (5, E2; ☎ 316 0101; www.dubaitennischampionships.com; Al-Garhoud)
Emirates Golf Club (4, A2; ☎ 347 3222; Interchange No 5, Sheikh Zayed Rd)
Nad al-Sheba Club (5, D3; ☎ 336 3666; www.nadalshebaclub.com; off Oud Metha Rd, Nad al-Sheba District, 5km south of Dubai centre)
Sharjah Cricket Stadium (5, F2; ☎ 06-532 2991; 2nd Industrial Rd, Industrial Area 5, Sharjah)

Sleeping

Dubai is a city that has hotel stars in its eyes. Perhaps no city in the world holds truer to the ethos of 'the more you pay, more you get' than Dubai. As you go up in stars the properties get more and more interesting and, in many cases, offer better value. Business hotels such as **Emirates Towers** (p70) are world class, staying at the iconic **Burj Al Arab** (p68) earns you unlimited bragging rights, and a night at **Mina A' Salam** (p68) is the stuff of *The Thousand and One Nights*. And there's plenty more to come – Dubai has a couple of dozen ostentatious four- and five-star properties due for completion before 2008, see p72.

ROOM RATES

These categories indicate the cost per night of a standard double room in high season, including the 10% municipal tax and 10% service charge.

Deluxe	>Dh1400
Top End	Dh700–1400
Midrange	Dh300–699
Budget	<Dh300

The sheer number of hotels in Dubai appears daunting, but working out where to stay is straightforward. If your aim is to relax and catch some rays, stay at one of the beach resorts along Jumeirah Beach, which are mainly five-star. If you're interested in heritage and culture, shopping and souqs, the city hotels of Deira and Bur Dubai will suit, with everything from one to five stars. If you're doing business in Dubai, there are excellent business hotels in all parts of the city, but due to the traffic it's recommended that you choose one close to where you need to be. Most hotels in Dubai are very kid-friendly and the facilities offered are generally in line with other parts of the world. Wheelchair access is generally excellent in the deluxe and top-end hotels. We've noted where access is limited or only fair. All hotels listed have air conditioning.

The hotel prices we've quoted are the hotels' published, high-season rack rates – which you're highly unlikely to pay. During summer, tourism numbers drop substantially and so do the room rates, often up to 40% of the published rate. Most hotels publish these specials on their websites. Conversely, for the peak periods and when there's an international sporting event or conference in town, Dubai actually runs out of hotel rooms, so you need to book well in advance.

Burj al Arab (the Arabian Tower, p68): an icon from just about any angle

DELUXE

Burj Al Arab (4, D1)

If you're the kind of traveller that name-drops hotels where they've stayed, this one's a must – after all, how many self-appointed seven-star hotels are there in the world? Its ostentatious opulence will leave you reeling, as will the unbeatable views from the two-storey suites, but the interior has no definitive style – unless 'over the top' qualifies as a style – and it bears little relation to the sleek exterior. With 202 suites and more than 1200 staff, service is never going to be anything less than personal and, while the bar snacks are brilliant, we've never been blown away by a meal here. See (p10) for more on this Dubai icon.

☎ 301 7777 ☐ www .burj-al-arab.com ✉ Jumeirah Rd, Jumeirah
☐ ✗ ☒ ⚹ ⚹

Jumeirah Beach Hotel (4, D1)

This huge wave-shaped hotel serves a diverse clientele; from beachcombing families to conference-goers pretending that staying here is somehow related to work. With more than 600 large and well-equipped rooms it's a vast resort, but the amenities offered disperses the masses to mostly water-based pursuits such as hanging on the private beach or taking a swimsuit-challenging ride at the adjacent Wild Wadi Waterpark (p29).

☎ 348 0000 ☐ www .jumeirahbeachhotel.com ✉ Jumeirah Rd, Jumeirah
☐ ✗ ☒ ⚹ ⚹

Le Meridien Grosvenor House (4, A1)

Dubai's newest Meridien plays the elegant and understated role to the hilt. It feels more city than seafaring with its exquisite cream and brown décor, spacious rooms (all with Gulf views) and excellent service. However, if you're desperate to feel the sand between your toes, take the shuttle to Le Royal Meridien Beach Resort. You'll want to return for dinner, though, as there are plenty of good eateries as well as a Buddha Bar (p60).

☎ 399 8888 ☐ www.gros venorhouse.lemeridien.com ✉ West Marina Beach, Jumeirah ☐ ✗ ☒ ⚹ ⚹

Le Royal Meridien Beach Resort (4, A1)

While this stately resort consists of three seemingly disconnected buildings, it's tied together neatly by the time-honoured Meridien landscaping and pools fronted by a vast private beach. It's a very relaxing resort, with large, well-appointed rooms, a lovely 'Roman' spa and a wide range of dining options on offer. Land-view rooms were affected by the work at Dubai Marina at the time of research.

☎ 399 5555 ☐ www .leroyalmeridien-dubai.com ✉ Al-Sufouh Rd, Jumeirah
☐ ✗ ☒ ⚹ ⚹

Mina A' Salam (4, C1)

The first hotel completed as part of the impressive Madinat Jumeirah resort, this 'harbour of peace' is a gorgeous slice of old Arabia. The elegantly designed

Ritz-Carlton (opposite)

rooms feature balconies and views over the harbour and the Arabian Gulf. With its excellent shopping and great restaurants, Souq Madinat Jumeirah (p39) is part of the complex as is a Six Senses Spa (p27), making this resort exceptionally difficult to leave.

☎ 366 8888 ☐ www .madinatjumeirah.com ✉ Al-Sufouh Rd, Jumeirah
☐ ✗ ☒ ⚹ ⚹

One&Only Royal Mirage (4, A1)

Despite the new Al-Qasr and Mina A' Salam upping the Arabian themed–resort stakes, this is arguably still the most romantic resort on the beach strip. The resort consists of three separate hotels, the Palace, the Arabian Court and the Residence & Spa, each more ornate (and expensive) than the last. Facilities are first-rate throughout and it's hard to beat a night that consists of the Rooftop (p60) drinks, dinner at Tagine (p57) and dancing at Kasbar (p61).

☎ 399 9999 ☐ www .oneandonlyresorts.com

✉ Al-Sufouh Rd, Jumeirah
🖥 ✂ 🏊 🚭 ♿

Park Hyatt Dubai (5, E2)
This new, elegant, Moroccan-styled, low-rise hotel has huge, well-appointed rooms all with wonderful views of Dubai Creek from the private balconies. The hotel, consisting of a series of wings, has a cool and airy feel throughout the public spaces and the rooms. It had just opened at the time of research, and the chic bars and restaurants of the hotel were already welcome additions to the Dubai scene.
☎ 602 1234 🖥 www .dubai.park.hyatt.com ✉ Dubai Creek Golf & Yacht Club, Deira
🖥 ✂ 🏊 🚭 ♿

Al-Qasr (4, C1)
Befitting its status as the centrepiece of the Madinat Jumeirah resort, this is a more opulent and stately hotel than Mina A' Salam, with slightly larger rooms. While all the rooms feature antique-style Arabian furnishings and private balconies, the ocean-facing deluxe rooms have views of the Arabian Gulf. Two kilometres of private beach, an amazing spa and preferential bookings for great restaurants such as Zheng He's (p57) make this a romantic place to relax.
☎ 366 8888 🖥 www .madinatjumeirah.com ✉ Al-Sufouh Rd, Jumeirah
🖥 ✂ 🏊 🚭 ♿

Ritz-Carlton (4, A1)
The Ritz-Carlton's first foray in the Middle East is a Mediterranean accented resort that won't disappoint fans of the Ritz-Carlton style. Generous-sized rooms, attractive gardens, excellent service – especially at La Baie (p55) restaurant – make it a good choice for those who like the clubby panache of the Ritz-Carlton chain.
☎ 399 4000 🖥 www .ritz-carlton.com ✉ Al-Sufouh Rd, Jumeirah
🖥 ✂ 🏊 🚭 ♿

TOP END

Al-Bustan Rotana (5, E2)
Apart from the lobby, it's not the most impressive hotel in the looks department, but it makes up for it with its convenient airport access, excellent facilities and very friendly service; the rooms are well equipped but uninspired. Head out to dinner at the Blue Elephant, (p49) and then check out the popular Oxygen nightclub (p62). There is wheelchair access, but it's limited.
☎ 282 0000 🖥 www .rotana.com ✉ Casablanca Rd, Deira 🖥 ✂ 🏊 🚭 ♿

Dusit Dubai (3, C3)
Another ingredient in the architectural soup that is Sheikh Zayed Rd is the distinct upside-down letter 'Y' shape of this elegant hotel. The Thai-style décor is chic, the service excellent and the outlook just gets better and better as you head skyward, concluding with spectacular views from the rooftop

IN THE MOOD FOR ARABIAN ROMANCE
Dubai Desert Conservation Reserve's **Al Maha Desert Resort & Spa** (1, B4; ☎ 303 4224; www.al-maha.com; 45km from Dubai; 🖥 🏊 ♿) is named after the oryx (see the boxed text, p76) it breeds so successfully. The eco-resort's luxurious stand-alone tent-roofed suites have chilled private pools and vistas of peach-coloured dunes dotted with beautiful white oryx. Wheelchair access is available to one suite only. There are wildlife drives and sunset camel rides (with champagne!), but Al Maha excels at the romantic rather than the social. Private vehicles, visitors and children aren't allowed and candle-lit in-suite dining is popular. If you can't rekindle a romance here, it's over.

Emirates Towers (below)

pool. Book Benjarong (p53) restaurant for a memorable Thai feast. Wheelchair access is limited.

☎ 343 3333 🖳 www.dusit.com ✉ Sheikh Zayed Rd, next to Interchange No 1 🖳 ✕ 🖙 ♿

Emirates Towers (3, D3)
While this is arguably the best business hotel in the Middle East, there's plenty to entertain those who are staying with more relaxing things in mind. Located in the shorter of the two towers, the rooms are sizeable, the service is excellent and the foyer is also one of Dubai's best people-watching locations. There's a chic shopping centre, some great restaurants, and a visit to the lofty Vu's bar (p54) via the glass elevator is a must-do.

☎ 330 0000 🖳 www.emiratestowershotel.com ✉ Sheikh Zayed Rd 🖳 ✕ 🖙 🖤 ♿

Fairmont (3, E3)
Another contemporary Sheikh Zayed Rd hotel that keeps both business- and

pleasure-seeking guests happy with excellent facilities and outstanding service. The comfortable and well-appointed standard rooms are great; for a treat there are opulent Arabic– or minimalist Japanese–style rooms to choose from. It's also home to an excellent spa, the Exchange Grill (p54) restaurant and the happening Tangerine (p62) nightclub.

☎ 332 5555 🖳 www.fairmont.com ✉ Sheikh Zayed Rd 🖳 ✕ 🖙 🖤 ♿

Grand Hyatt Dubai (5, E2)
With 674 rooms, this is a grand Hyatt in every sense of the word. All the amenities are on a grand scale, with 14 busy bars and restaurants (including the excellent Indochine, p52). There are also acres of gardens and several pools. The rooms are tastefully decorated with Arabian touches and the public areas of the hotel are breathtaking.

☎ 317 1234 🖳 www.dubai.grand.hyatt.com ✉ Al-Qataiyat Rd, Bur Dubai 🖳 ✕ 🖙 🖤 ♿

Hilton Dubai Creek (2, D4)
The coolest creekside address, the Carlos Ott–designed lines offer guests relief from the over-the-top opulence elsewhere. The rooms are spacious and the beds divine – nice to crawl back to after a degustation demolition at the hotel's wonderful restaurant, Verre (p50). Book a room on a high floor with a stunning view of the bustling Creek and get in early for a sunbed at the rooftop pool.

☎ 227 1111 🖳 www.hilton.com ✉ Baniyas Rd, Deira 🖳 ✕ 🖙 ♿

Hyatt Regency Dubai (2, E1)
After a stylish face-lift, this senior citizen is looking decidedly youthful. The executive suites have been renovated and all rooms are comfortable; those on the upper floors offer great views of the Gulf. There are handy facilities such as shops, restaurants, cinemas and even an indoor ice-skating rink. Well situated for souq shopping raids.

☎ 209 1234 🖳 www.dubai.regency.hyatt.com

DREAMY DESERT ESCAPE

Dubai has a sublime desert escape in **Bab al-Shams Desert Resort & Spa** (1, B4; ☎ 832 6699; www.babalshams.com; Margham; 🖳 ✕ 🖙 🖤 ♿). The labyrinthine desert medina is ideal for relaxation; the Arabian-style rooms are spacious and it's worth finding space in your bag for the Dead Sea toiletries! The pool is the focus of daytime activity, with attention turning to Al-Sarab bar for sunset *sheesha*, a falconry display and prettily decorated camels positioned on the horizon for postcard snapshots. Al-Hadheerah desert restaurant offers the full Arabian experience while Al-Forsan serves refined international cuisine.

STOPOVER SPECIALS

OK, so you have 24 hours or less? No problem. Here are the best hotels for a stopover, convenient for both sight-seeing and the airport. Just watch the shopping or you'll end up making a mockery of the baggage allowance.

- Al-Bustan Rotana (p69)
- Hilton Dubai Creek (opposite)
- Shangri-La (right)
- Novotel (p73)
- Ibis (p72)

✉ off Al-Khaleej Rd, Deira

Le Meridien Mina Seyahi Resort (4, A1)

This stylish and delightfully landscaped resort is perfect for sun-worshippers, with excellent water-sports facilities and a gorgeous pool area complete with a peril-ously seductive wet bar. The standard rooms are rightly called deluxe rooms, given their size, and sea-facing rooms are recommended. The eateries are good and the Barasti Bar (p59) is one of the best beach bars in Dubai.

☎ 399 3333 💻 www .lemeridien-minaseyahi.com

✉ Al-Sufouh Rd, Jumeirah

Shangri-La (3, C3)

Cool and understated, Shangri-La is a smart choice that attracts low-key celebrities who have a sense of style. The ultra-stylish and curvaceous rooms all feature stunning views of either the city or the sea. The hotel also boasts all the expected business facilities as well as a well-equipped health club and the noteworthy Hoi An (p53) restaurant.

☎ 343 8888 💻 www .shangri-la.com
✉ Sheikh Zayed Rd

Sheraton Dubai Creek (2, D4)

After an extensive renova-tion, the Sheraton Dubai Creek now takes full advantage of its awesome position, smack bang on the Creek. There are numerous room options available, some with amazing creek vistas, but the inexplicable Japanese-themed rooms really mess with our minds. Good food outlets and a comfortable (weather per-mitting!) walking distance to the souqs. Wheelchair access is limited.

☎ 228 1111 💻 www .starwoodhotels.com
✉ Baniyas Rd, Deira

Le Merdian Mina Seyahi Resort (above) is perfect for sun worshippers

Time out for reflection at Sheraton Dubai Creek (p71)

MIDRANGE

Crowne Plaza Hotel
(3, D3)
This Sheikh Zayed Rd stalwart is showing its age, but hosts a range of facilities that keep business and leisure travellers loyal. It's a large complex, complete with a shopping centre, bars and restaurants including the venerable Trader Vic's (p54) and ever-popular Zinc (p62) nightclub.
☎ 331 1111 🖳 www .dubai.crowneplaza.com ✉ Sheikh Zayed Rd
🖳 ✕ 🐟 ♿ ⛱

Four Points Sheraton
(2, B3)
This small, somewhat unremarkable four-star Sheraton is geared towards the business traveller, but its position makes it a good choice for shopping and wandering around Dubai's heritage areas. The hotel is also home to the excellent Antique Bazaar Indian restaurant (p51). There is wheelchair access, but it's limited.
☎ 397 7444 🖳 www .fourpoints.com ✉ Khalid bin al-Waleed Rd, Bur Dubai
🖳 ✕ 🐟 ♿ ⛱

Ibis (3, D3)
Surprisingly stylish, this hotel's groovy lobby perhaps makes promises the small rooms can't keep. It's aimed at trade-show and convention goers, and at this price point it's fantastic value for a hotel on the Sheikh Zayed strip.
☎ 318 7000 🖳 www .ibishotel.com ✉ behind World Trade Centre, Sheikh Zayed Rd 🖳 ✕ 🐟 ♿

Mövenpick Hotel Bur Dubai (2, A6)
While the Mövenpick chain doesn't set hearts aflutter, this is a great choice for shopping expeditions and airport access. As usual with Mövenpick, business facilities are excellent, there's wi-fi all round and the rooftop pool and fitness centre are first-rate.
☎ 336 6000 🖳 www .moevenpick-hotels .com ✉ 19 St, Bur Dubai
✕ 🐟 ♿ ⛱

OPENING SOON!
Hotel openings are virtually a monthly event in Dubai. Here's a list of the more attention-grabbing hotels coming soon, notable for their name, location, or just sheer bravado. For the Kempinski Hotel Mall of the Emirates, see p24.
Armani Hotel (2008; www.armanihotels.com) The new Armani chain's first hotel will be located in the world's tallest building, the Burj Dubai (p23).
Hydropolis (2007; www.hydropolis.com) Claustrophobics best not even glance at a brochure for the world's first underwater hotel. There's the promise of the healing power of water; if that doesn't work there's a cosmetic surgery clinic planned.
Palazzo Dubai (2008) It's fitting that Versace's second hotel property should be located in Dubai, when the first was at Australia's glitzy Gold Coast. This one will feature temperature-controlled sand.

Novotel (3, D3)

A no-nonsense Novotel situated behind the Sheikh Zayed strip, it's kept busy with the business, trade and convention set along with Ibis. The modern design and decent food are both welcome and, while there's not much here to keep nonbusiness guests hanging about, it's only a short taxi ride to Dubai's sights and shopping and the city's latest hotspot, Lotus One (p60), is next door.
☎ 332 0000 ⌨ www.novotel.com ✉ behind World Trade Centre

TOP FIVE DUBAI SLEEPS
- Best city hotel – Hilton Dubai Creek (p70)
- Best Arabian hotel – Mina A' Salam (p68)
- Best beach resort – One&Only Royal Mirage (p68)
- Best business hotel – Emirates Towers (p70)
- Best escape hotel – Al Maha Resort (p69)

Riviera Hotel (2, D3)

Right on the Creek and close to the atmospheric souqs, this hotel is worthwhile if you can score one of the creek-facing rooms with simply brilliant views. Despite a refurbishment, the hotel is still a little frumpy looking but it has fine facilities and an excellent Deira location. Wheelchair access is limited.
☎ 222 2131 ⌨ www.rivierahotel-dubai.com ✉ Baniyas Rd, Deira

Rydges Plaza (3, E2)

This Aussie chain is decidedly old-fashioned, but it's a short cab ride from beach and city hot spots. The service is friendly, the restaurants are notable and complimentary beach and airport transfers help sweeten the deal. Wheelchair access is limited.
☎ 398 2222 ⌨ www.rydges.com ✉ Satwa Roundabout

XVA (2, C2)

This small hotel is unique in Dubai, located in one of the Bastakia Quarter's (p9) recently restored houses. The sparse rooms, arranged around a central courtyard housing an art gallery and café, are furnished in a minimalist Oriental style. There's limited wheelchair access.
☎ 353 5383 ✉ xva@xvagallery.com ✉ behind Basta Art Café, Al-Musallah Roundabout, Bur Dubai

BUDGET

Dubai Youth Hostel (5, F2)

The only youth hostel in Dubai is a little way from the action, but it's playing to a captive audience of budget travellers. Stick to the new wing, with its comfortable single and double rooms. Accessible by buses 3, 13, 17 and 31. Wheelchair access is fair, but not extensive.
☎ 298 8161 ⌨ uaeyha@emirates.net.ae ✉ Al-Nahda Rd

Al-Hijaz Heritage Motel (2, C1)

Smack bang in the middle of Deira's heritage area and right next to the Al-Ahmadiya School (p20), this basic hotel offers up the rare chance to stay in a heritage-style house. While it's the kind of place you'd love to renovate a little further, the rooms are huge, clean and a bargain – so book well in advance. There is wheelchair access but it's limited.
☎ 225 0085 ⌨ alhijazmotel.com ✉ next to Al-Ahmadiya School, Deira

Hotel Florida (2, D2)

Right next to the Deira (Al-Sabkha) bus station, this hotel offers small, clean rooms and is better than you'd reasonably expect at this price point. Wheelchair access is fair.
☎ 226 8888 ⌨ www.floridahotels.co.ae ✉ Al-Sabkha Rd, Deira

About Dubai

HISTORY
Early Settlement
Archaeological remains in the area around the city show evidence of humans as far back as 8000 BC. Until 3000 BC the area supported nomadic herders, who fished on the coast during winter and relocated inland with their herds during summer. Agriculture developed with the cultivation of date palms around 2500 BC, providing food and materials for building and weaving.

The next major habitation of the area was by the Sassanids who ruled in Persia from AD 224 to 636. The Umayyads supplanted the Sassanids in the 7th century, bringing the Arabic language to the region and joining it with the Islamic world. During this period, maritime trade in the Gulf expanded due to its location on the major trade routes between the Mediterranean Sea and the Indian Ocean.

European Presence
In the late 16th century Portugal became the first European power to take advantage of the region's lucrative trade routes with India and the Far East. Dispirited by the monopolistic, well-armed Portuguese traders, local tribes took refuge in land-locked oases such as Liwa and Al-Ain.

The French and the Dutch infiltrated the area in the 17th and 18th centuries, aspiring to control the trading routes to the east. The British were equally intent on protecting the sea route to India, and in 1766 the Dutch gave way to Britain's East India Company, which had established Gulf trading links in 1616.

The Trucial Coast
When the powerful Bani Yas tribal leaders moved from the Liwa Oasis to Abu Dhabi in 1833, about 800 tribe members split off and settled by the creek in Bur Dubai instead. Led by Maktoum bin Butti, this established the Al-Maktoum dynasty of Dubai. Throughout the 19th century Dubai remained an enclave of fishermen, pearl divers, Bedouin, Indian and

Indulge those Lawrence of Arabia fantasies at the edge of Rub'Al-Khali (the Empty Quarter)

THE AL-MAKTOUM DYNASTY

The ruling family of Dubai are chronic overachievers. Sheikh Maktoum bin Rashid al-Maktoum is the ruler of Dubai as well as being vice president and prime minister of the UAE. His brother, Sheikh Hamdan, is the deputy ruler of Dubai and the federal minister of finance and industry. Their uncle, Sheikh Ahmed bin Saeed al-Maktoum, is the chairman of Emirates Airlines (see also the boxed text, p65).

Sheikh Mohammed, the third brother, is the Crown Prince of Dubai and defence minister of the UAE. Perhaps the most visible and charismatic face of the ruling family, he's constantly in the public eye with his myriad ambitious development projects (see also the boxed text, p36).

Persian merchants. In 1892, the British reinforced their power through 'exclusive agreements' with the sheikhs. Because of these agreements, or 'truces', Europeans referred to the area as the Trucial Coast, a name retained until federation. In 1894 Dubai's ruler, Sheikh Maktoum bin Hasher al-Maktoum, permitted tax exemption for foreign traders and the free port of Dubai was born – existing to this day.

The Expanding City

By the turn of the 20th century, Dubai was a well-established town with a population of about 10,000. The city survived some lean years after the collapse of the vitally important pearling industry in 1929. After a brief attempt at a consultative government in 1939 (see the boxed text, p77), Sheikh Rashid bin Saeed al-Maktoum ef-

A fresh perspective from the water

fectively took over from his father, Sheikh Saeed and quickly bolstered the emirate's position as the key trading hub in the lower Gulf. In 1951 the Trucial States Council was founded, bringing together the leaders of what would become the UAE.

Recent History

Oil was discovered in Dubai in 1966, and the speed of Dubai's growth multiplied when export began in 1969. As part of its departure from the region in 1968, Britain attempted to create a state that encompassed the Trucial States, Bahrain and Qatar. Bahrain and Qatar decided to move to their own independence, but the leaders of Abu Dhabi and Dubai strengthened their commitment to a single state. The federation of the United Arab Emirates was born on 2 December 1971; it consisted of the emirates of Dubai, Abu Dhabi, Ajman, Fujairah, Sharjah and Um Al Quwain; Ras Al Kaimah joined in 1972. Under the agreement, the emirs approved a formula whereby Abu Dhabi and Dubai (in that order) would carry the most weight in the federation but would leave each emir largely autonomous. Sheikh Zayed of Abu Dhabi became the president of the UAE and Sheikh Rashid of Dubai became vice president.

Sheikh Rashid died in 1990 after a long illness and was succeeded by the eldest of his four sons, Sheikh Maktoum bin Rashid al-Maktoum, who had been regent for his father during his illness. The Crown Prince and third son of the dynasty, Sheikh Mohammed bin Rashid al-Maktoum is perhaps the most visible of Dubai's leaders; see the boxed text, p75.

ENVIRONMENT

Dubai was originally a flat *sabkha* (salt-crusted coastal plain) broken only by clumps of desert grasses and a small area of hardy mangroves at the inland end of the Creek. There are several well-established parks and gardens around the city, but Dubai is increasingly a concrete jungle.

Dubai is a clean city, although air pollution from the ever-growing traffic is becoming a major issue. Despite community education, rubbish is left on beaches, in parks or thrown out of car windows, and a large team of workers keeps the city spotless. Dubai generates one of the highest per capita volumes of waste in the world, and the Emirates Environmental Group has opened recycling centres around the city to manage it.

Over the years the damage caused by offshore oil spills has prompted a concerted effort by government agencies to monitor and control marine pollution, which also threatens the city's vital desalination plants.

TAKING BACK THE DESERT

Dubai seems more interested in theme parks than national parks, but in fact the emirate's largest project to date has involved rehabilitating the desert. **Al Maha Desert Resort & Spa** (p69) opened in 1999 on land allocated to Emirates Airlines, and its success led to an environmental audit in 2000. A conservation proposal was approved in 2002, and the Dubai Desert Conservation Reserve (DDCR) now encompasses nearly 5% of Dubai emirate.

Replantings of native flora have enabled reintroduction of the descendants of a herd of Arabian oryx (a large variety of antelope) along with several other species. The result has been a stunning success and it's heartening that Dubai has an attraction whose appeal is in simply watching herds of graceful oryxes graze.

RETURNING FIRE

Sheikh Saeed al-Maktoum was never happy with the implementation of a consultative council to oversee Dubai's affairs, and was suspicious of the motives of some of his relatives, so he ordered Bedouin guests to attack the council during his son's wedding on 29 March 1939.

One of the chief dissenters (a cousin) and his followers then settled in Sharjah – a little too close for the Sheikh's comfort. A half-hearted battle broke out between Dubai and Sharjah and, with little ammunition and not much more enthusiasm, rival forces resorted to using ancient muzzle-loading cannons.

During battle Imperial Airways continued to refuel its flying boats on Dubai Creek and send the passengers over to the fort at Sharjah for lunch. For this operation a truce was called so the passengers could eat in peace.

GOVERNMENT & POLITICS

Power in Dubai rests with the ruling family, the Al-Maktoums (see the boxed text, p75). Though the UAE has a federal government, each of the rulers (emirs) is absolutely sovereign within his own emirate. The Supreme Council is the national forum and the highest legislative body in the country, comprising the seven emirs. The Supreme Council also elects one of the emirs to a five-year term as the country's president. In practice, however, this role has been filled unchallenged by the emir of

A model of Jebel Ali Palm Islands (p80)

Abu Dhabi. After the much mourned passing of the nation's founder, Sheikh Zayed, in 2004, the presidency went to his son, Sheikh Khalifa, without incident.

There is also a cabinet and the posts within it are also distributed among the emirates. The Dubai Municipality is effectively the local government for the Emirate, handling everything from economic planning to rubbish collection. There are no political parties or general elections in Dubai.

ECONOMY

Dubai is the second richest emirate in the UAE, after Abu Dhabi. Dubai's dwindling oil and gas reserves make up only 7% of its GDP, and Dubai prudently uses the revenue to create the infrastructure for trade, manufacturing and tourism.

The re-export trade in Dubai makes up about 80% of the UAE's

Tailoring the economy

total re-export business, with exports mainly going to other Middle Eastern states. With its tax breaks and strong infrastructure, Dubai has been very successful in enticing global companies to make the city their base in the Middle East.

Dubai's per capita income is around Dh60,000 per annum – a figure far in excess of the wages earned by expat labourers sweating it out for Dh500 to Dh1000 a month. While it's unlikely that we'll see masses of Emiratis competing for bricklaying duties anytime soon, the government has made attempts to 'Emiratise' the workforce by placing nationals in the public workforce and imposing local-employee quotas on some industries.

SOCIETY & CULTURE
Identity & Lifestyle

Estimates put Dubai's population at more than 1.2 million, but only around 15% of the population of Dubai are Emiratis. The expatriate community makes up the rest of the population, and Dubai is one of the most multicultural cities in the world.

Dubai's tolerant and relaxed society hosts scores of different lifestyles coexisting with little friction. For Emiratis, day-to-day activities, relationships, diet and dress are dictated very much by religion and tradition. While gender roles are slowly changing, overall traditions are still adhered to; men engage with the outside world, and women control the domestic sphere.

The amount of disposable income earned by expatriates dictates their lifestyle. Academics, media, health and IT professionals have roughly the same gross income as they would at home, but packages often include free housing and other benefits – as well as no income tax.

DID YOU KNOW?

- Dubai attracted around 5 million visitors in 2004, but plans on reaching 15 million by 2010
- to support predicted visitor numbers, dozens of hotels are being constructed
- rumour has it that Dubai is preparing a bid for the 2016 summer Olympic Games
- Dubai's population has nearly doubled since 1995, it now stands at around 1.2 million
- men outnumber women by 2:1 and women comprise only 15% of the workforce

In the cleaning station of Dubai's fish souq

Workers from India, Pakistan and the Philippines make up the largest part of Dubai's huge service sector. These workers stand to earn much more in Dubai, but living conditions and working hours are generally tough.

Etiquette/Dos & Don'ts

Dubai is a remarkably liberal Muslim state. A good way to help keep it that way is to dress reasonably conservatively (see p26) and refrain from public displays of affection when Emiratis are present.

If you are meeting Emiratis, it's polite to shake men's hands, but don't extend your hand to Emirati women unless they do so first.

ARTS
Visual Arts

Dubai's visual arts scene is starting to flourish. Most art shown in established galleries was produced by expats, but the local work now being shown is more interesting. In the past, themes reflected the history, heritage and culture of Dubai, whereas more artists are now experimenting in abstract and mixed media forms. Mohammad Kanoo recently exhibited his pop art to glowing reviews. Several female Emirati artists have gained well-deserved attention, including Sheikha Hessah (Sheikh Maktoum's daughter). Galleries such as the **Third Line** (p21) are showing adventurous work; however, credit for the invigoration of the scene goes to Sheikha Hoor al-Qasimi, director of the outstanding **Sharjah International Biennial** (p59).

Poetry & Literature

There is some wonderful Arabic-language literature, yet little is available in English. Only some of Mohammed al-Murr's short stories have been translated. Iranian expat Marian Behnam's *Heirloom: Evening Tales from the East* retells folk tales from the 1920s to 1940s, translated from Bastaki, her mother tongue. There is a lively children's literature scene in Dubai: Julia Johnson's delightful illustrated books such as *A is for Arabia* make super kid's souvenirs.

It's poetry that permeates the cultural, intellectual and everyday life of Emiratis. In Bedouin culture, poetry is prized and Emiratis spontaneously recite it with their friends at social occasions and public events. Young people publish their own poetry, particularly romantic poems, on websites and in magazines. There are scores of well-known local male poets who experiment with classical Arabic poetry, combining it with other styles, and a handful of female poets write as well. The Jebel Ali Palm Island project features small islands shaped out of Sheikh Mohammed's poetry.

Cinema

While the Emirati film industry has been slow to develop, 2005 saw the premiere of the country's first feature film, a light-hearted lost-in-the-desert flick by Hani al-Shaibhani. Only a few years ago there was just a small grassroots film culture, most notably through the Higher Colleges of Technology's communications programme, but there are now two film festivals and construction of Film City is underway.

Dubai local Masoud Amralla Ali Ali can be given most of the credit for developing local talent by starting the Emirates Film Competition. In 2005 the awards primarily went to young women from the Abu Dhabi and Dubai Women's Colleges, who produced strong local narratives about their everyday life. Amralla's Middle East film programme for the inaugural Dubai International Film Festival (2004) was exceptional; however, the rest of the selection consisted of uninspiring films and media attention was focused on imported Hollywood stars.

Dance & Song

Traditional music and dance are performed at weddings and social gatherings. Most likely brought to the Gulf by East African slaves, the *liwa* is danced to a loud drumbeat, and traditionally sung in Swahili. A typical Bedouin dance celebrating courage, strength and unity, the *ayyalah* is performed througout the Gulf. Visitors can see traditional dance and music during Dubai Shopping Festival, on National Day, and at the Heritage Village during winter.

The more interesting contemporary Arab music, from collectives such as Oryx, Blue Bedouin, and Lemonada, has been produced at Dubai Media City. The fusion of

Setting the rhythm for tranditional dance

sounds is often the result of the diverse backgrounds of the musicians. While some Arab bands perform everything from metal to punk, the music you're most likely to hear on the radio is *khaleeji,* the traditional Gulf style recognisable to those familiar with Arabic pop music.

Directory

ARRIVAL & DEPARTURE

Air
DUBAI INTERNATIONAL AIRPORT
Dubai's **airport** (2, F6; general inquiries ☎ 224 5555, flight inquiries ☎ 206 6666; www.dubaiairport.com) is the busiest in the Middle East and rightly renowned for its excellent duty-free shopping. All major international airlines use Terminal 1, the main terminal; other carriers use the much smaller Terminal 2. There are left-luggage facilities at the airport.

Airport Access
The airport is about 5km southeast of the city centre. **Airport buses** (☎ 800 4848) run every 30 minutes to Deira (bus 401) and Bur Dubai (bus 402), and the fare is Dh3. However, the easiest option is to take one of the Dubai Transport taxis from the arrivals area. A ride to the Deira souq area is about Dh30, Bur Dubai around Dh40, while to the Jumeirah hotels the fare starts at around Dh60.

Travel Documents
PASSPORT
To enter Dubai your passport must have at least six months validity from the date of your arrival. Officially, you will be denied entry if your passport shows any evidence of travel to Israel, and Israeli passport holders are not permitted to enter.

VISAS
Visas valid for 60 days are available on arrival for citizens of most developed countries. These include all western European countries, Australia, Brunei, Canada, Hong Kong, Japan, Malaysia, New Zealand, Singapore, South Korea and the USA. No fee is charged for tourist visas.

Citizens of other Gulf Cooperative Council (GCC) countries do not need visas to enter the UAE. For citizens of other countries, a transit or tourist visa must be arranged through a sponsor. This can be a hotel, a company or a resident of the UAE. Most hotels charge about Dh200 to arrange a visa.

Customs & Duty Free
The duty-free allowances are 2000 cigarettes, 400 cigars or 2kg of loose tobacco and a reasonable amount of perfume, per person. There's also an allowance of 2L of wine and 2L of spirits for non-Muslims. No customs duties are applied to personal belongings.

GETTING AROUND
The best way of getting around Dubai is by taxi, as the planned light-rail system is some years off. Only hire a car if you are a confident driver who can handle Middle East traffic madness and you plan on taking a couple of day trips (p34). There is a public bus system, but slowly melting into a bus stop seat in 40˚C heat is not a great way to experience Dubai. Note that only major roads have names in Dubai – all minor roads have a confusing system of numbers. Most taxi drivers know the places you'll be going to in Dubai.

Taxi
Dubai has a large, modern fleet of metered taxis. The starting fare is Dh3 plus Dh1.43 per kilometre, rising to Dh3.50 plus Dh1.70 per kilometre between 10pm and 6am. Drivers will try to round up to the nearest Dh5, so keep some smaller notes (Dh5s and Dh10s) and coins handy. **Dubai Transport** (☎ 208 0808), with the cream-coloured fleet can provide wheelchair-accessible taxis if you book in advance.

Car
If you're planning on taking a day or overnight excursion from Dubai, hiring a car is the best way to do it; however, traffic congestion in Dubai can be a real problem at peak hours (7am to 9am and 5pm to 7pm).

Parking is plentiful and petrol is sold by the gallon (just over 4.5L). Regular petrol costs Dh4 per gallon and premium is Dh4.56.

ROAD RULES

Motorists drive on the right-hand side of the road in Dubai – most of the time – and you'll witness some spectacularly innovative driving so be aware at all times. The speed limit is 60km/h on city streets and 80km/h on major city roads, although traffic jams often render these irrelevant. On dual-lane highways around the UAE the speed limit is 120km/h and 100km/h on some sections. Dubai is teeming with speed cameras and fines start at Dh500. Car rental companies require customers to authorise the company to charge their credit card for fines incurred. It is compulsory to wear front seatbelts and it is illegal to use a hand-held mobile phone while driving, but in practice you'll find that both rules are ignored by many locals.

HIRE

It's best to hire from well-known companies for both insurance and safety reasons. Small vehicles, such as a Toyota Corolla, start at about Dh120 per day with another Dh20 to Dh25 for collision damage waiver (CDW) insurance. Most foreign driving licences are accepted in Dubai. Rental companies usually offer a chauffeur service, around Dh180 per eight hours.

Avis (☎ 295 7121; www.avis.com)
Budget (☎ 282 3030; www.budget.com)
Europcar (☎ 339 4433; www.europcar.com)
Hertz (☎ 282 4422; www.hertz-uae.com)

Abra

Scores of *abras* (small motorboats) cross the Creek from early morning until around midnight, taking two routes. See Map 2, for the normal routes, although at the time of writing these were altered slightly due to construction work. The fare is a measly 50 fils and the view from the water is unique.

Bus

Local buses operate out of the two main stations in Deira (2, D1) and Bur Dubai (2, B1). Numbers and routes are posted on the buses in English and Arabic. Fares are Dh1 to Dh3.50, depending on the distance. A free schedule and route map can be picked up from the main stations. For information call the 24-hour **Dubai Municipality hotline** (☎ 800 4848).

PRACTICALITIES

Business Hours

Business hours and working days are not fixed in Dubai. Government departments generally work from Saturday to Wednesday, 7.30am to 2.30pm, and private companies generally open for business from 8am to 5pm or from 9am to 6pm, but may take Friday to Saturday as the weekend or even Friday – the weekly Muslim holy day. Shopping malls are generally open 10am to 10pm and other shops 10am to 1pm and 4pm to 9pm. On Fridays most shops are shut in the morning and open around 1pm or 2pm.

Climate & When to Go

Dubai's year-round weather is warm and humid with a cloudless sky. The summer months (May to September) are extremely hot with daytime temperatures topping out in the low to mid-40s (Celsius). July and August are the hottest, with average daytime temperatures of around 43°C and up to 80% humidity. The sea temperature during these months is about 37°C – providing you survive the walk across the sand. Hotel swimming pools are tempera-

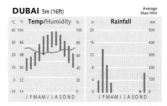

ture controlled so hoteliers don't boil their guests alive.

During October, November, March and April the weather is much more bearable, with daytime temperatures in the low to mid-30s. In winter (December to February) Dubai enjoys perfect weather with an average temperature of 24°C and a night-time average of 15°C.

It doesn't rain often, or heavily, but when it does (usually in December or January) getting around can suddenly become difficult as streets turn into rivers and traffic becomes chaotic. Drivers here are not used to wet road conditions, and the city planners decided Dubai didn't need a drainage system, so there are no gutter or stormwater drains. The average annual rainfall is about very low (it rains only five days a year on average), but rainfall varies widely from one year to the next. In winter there can be fog in the early mornings.

Sandstorms can occur during March and April, although Dubai is protected from the swirling dust and sand to some degree by its many tall buildings.

Consulates
Most countries have diplomatic representation in the UAE. Dubai is home to the consulates and one embassy (British); other embassies are in Abu Dhabi and are listed in the front pages of the Dubai phone book.
Australia (3, A3; ☎ 321 2444; Emarat Atrium, Sheikh Zayed Rd, Zabeel)
Canada (2, B3; ☎ 352 1717; 7th fl, United Bank Bldg, Khalid bin al-Waleed Rd, Bur Dubai)
France (3, D3; ☎ 332 9040; 18th fl, API World Tower, Sheikh Zayed Rd, Zabeel)
Germany (2, B4; ☎ 379 0002; 1st fl, Sharaf Bldg, Khalid bin al-Waleed Rd, near BurJuman Centre, Bur Dubai)
India (2, C4; ☎ 397 1222; 7B St, Bur Dubai)
Italy (3, E3; ☎ 331 4167; 17th fl, Dubai World Trade Centre, Sheikh Zayed Rd, Zabeel)

Netherlands (2, B3; ☎ 352 8700; 5th fl, ABN-Amro Bank Bldg, Khalid bin al-Waleed Rd, Bur Dubai)
South Africa (2, B4; ☎ 397 5222; 3rd fl, Sharaf Bldg, Khalid bin al-Waleed Rd, near BurJuman Centre, Bur Dubai)
UK (2, C3; ☎ 397 1070; Al-Seef Rd, Bur Dubai)
USA (3, E3; ☎ 311 6000; 21st fl, Dubai World Trade Centre, Sheikh Zayed Rd, Zabeel)

Disabled Travellers
Once outside the airport (which has decent facilities), Dubai is not a particularly disabled-friendly destination. **Dubai Transport** (☎ 208 0808) has taxis that can take wheelchairs. We have rated hotels that have good or excellent disabled access with a ⑤ symbol and no additional comment. Those with either a good or excellent rating have dedicated disabled rooms and good access throughout the hotel. Where there is disabled access but it is fair or limited, we have noted this in the review.

Electricity
British-style three-pin wall sockets are used, but most appliances sold in Dubai have two-pin plugs. Adaptors are inexpensive and available everywhere.

Voltage	220V
Frequency	50Hz
Cycle	AC
Plugs	British-style 3-pin

Emergencies
Outside the city's life-threatening driving style, Dubai is an extremely safe travel destination.

Ambulance	☎ 998/999
Electrical faults	☎ 991
Fire department	☎ 997
Police	☎ 999
Operator	☎ 181

Fitness

Dubai is a body-conscious city, especially for the club-going crowd. During the cooler months, the parks and beaches (p22) are popular venues for swimming and running; otherwise it's off to the air-conditioned, well-equipped health clubs dotted around the city. For spas and pampering see p27.

The deluxe and top-end hotels have health clubs, but standards vary widely. The facilities of the larger places include a gym, sauna, swimming pool, squash courts and tennis courts. Below is a selection of health clubs that accept casual visitors. All the clubs listed below have treadmills, bikes, step machines, rowing machines, free weights and resistance machines as well as massage, sauna and steam room.

Fitness Planet (3, E2; ☎ 398 9030; Al-Hana Centre, Satwa)
Inter-Fitness (2, D3; ☎ 222 7171; InterContinental Hotel, Baniyas Rd, Deira)
Nautilus Academy (2, B3; ☎ 397 4117; Al-Mussalla Towers, Khalid bin al-Waleed Rd, Bur Dubai)

Gay & Lesbian Travellers

Homosexuality is illegal in the UAE and can incur a jail term. Dubai makes a huge effort to promote itself as a tolerant, safe tourist destination, but open displays of homosexuality can land you in trouble. Note that any gay-focused websites are blocked in the UAE.

Health
IMMUNISATIONS

There are no vaccination requirements for entering Dubai and the UAE.

PRECAUTIONS

The biggest concerns when visiting Dubai are dehydration and sunstroke. For visitors from a mild climate, the ferocious heat and humidity of Dubai can take its toll quickly. High factor sun creams, a hat and decent sunglasses are essential. Dubai's tap water is drinkable, but most locals drink bottled water.

MEDICAL SERVICES

Travel insurance is a must to cover any medical treatment you may need while in Dubai. Visitors are eligible for emergency medical care but will be charged for it; generally the standard of medical services is good. If your need is not urgent, ask your consulate for the latest list of recommended doctors and dentists. The following government hospitals have emergency departments:
Al-Wasl Hospital (5, E2; ☎ 324 1111; Oud Metha Rd, south of Al-Qataiyat Rd, Zabeel)
New Dubai Hospital (2, F2; ☎ 222 9171; Abu Baker al-Siddiq Rd, near the corner of Al-Khaleej Rd, Hor al-Anz)
Rashid Hospital (2, B6; ☎ 337 4000; off Oud Metha Rd, near Al-Maktoum Bridge, Bur Dubai)

DENTAL SERVICES

There are excellent dental services in Dubai. For emergency (24-hour) dental treatment, phone 050 551 7177.

PHARMACIES

There are pharmacies on just about every street in Dubai. See the *Gulf News* for a list of pharmacies that are open 24 hours on that day or if you need to get to a pharmacy urgently, call ☎ 223 2323, a hotline that will tell you the location of the nearest open pharmacy.

Holidays

Secular holidays in Dubai include New Year's Day (1 January) and National Day (2 December). Religious holidays follow the Islamic calendar and approximate dates are listed, but the exact dates are determined by the sighting of the moon. Eid al-Fitr is a three-day celebration after Ramadan (p52), and Eid al-Adha is a four-day celebration after the main pilgrimage to Mecca, or haj.

Islamic New Year	31 January 2006
	20 January 2007
	10 January 2008

Prophet's Birthday	11 April 2006
	31 March 2007
Ramadan	24 September 2006
	13 September 2007
Eid al-Fitr	24 October 2006
	13 October 2007
Eid al-Adha	31 December 2006
	20 December 2007

Internet
INTERNET ACCESS
Etisalat is effectively the sole provider of Internet access in Dubai although deregulation is underway. Most hotels offer Internet access to their guests, with broadband and wi-fi fast becoming the norm. For those travelling with wi fi–equipped laptops or PDAs, Etisalat has a new 'iZone' wi-fi service and wherever you see the iZone logo you can buy prepaid cards (starting at Dh15 for one hour) and start wireless surfing. Most shopping centres and the insidious Starbucks cafés have iZone.

There are a few specialist Internet cafés around the city, and you'll find small cafés in the shopping centres that have terminals. Rates are around Dh10 to Dh15 per hour and reliable Internet cafés include:

Al-Jalssa Internet Café (2, B3; ☎ 351 4617; Al-Ain Shopping Centre, Al-Mankhool Rd; ☾ 9am-1am)
French Connection (3, C3; ☎ 343 8311; Wafa Tower, Sheikh Zayed Rd; ☾ 9am-1am)

USEFUL WEBSITES
Lonely Planet's website (www.lonelyplanet .com) offers a speedy link to many websites on Dubai. Others to try include:
Dubai Tourism & Commerce Marketing (www.dubaitourism.ae)
Sheikh Mohammed bin Rashid al-Maktoum (www.sheikhmohammed.com)
UAE Interact (www.uaeinteract.com)

Metric System
The metric system is used in the UAE, although Imperial measurements are widely understood.

Money
CURRENCY
The UAE dirham (Dh) is divided into 100 fils. Notes come in denominations of Dh5, 10, 20, 50, 100, 200, 500 and 1000. There are Dh1, 50 fils, 25 fils, 10 fils and 5 fils coins (the latter two are rarely used). The coins only show the denomination in Arabic, so it's a great way to learn, turn to p87 for the numerals.

EXCHANGE RATES
The UAE dirham is fully convertible and – for better or worse depending where you're coming from – pegged to the US dollar at a rate of Dh3.6725. Exchange rates are much better in the city than at the airport.

Australia	
A$1	Dh2.8
Canada	
C$1	Dh2.9
Euro	
€1	Dh4.7
New Zealand	
NZ$1	Dh2.7
South Africa	
ZAR1	Dh0.6
UK	
£1	Dh6.9
USA	
US$1	Dh3.6

TRAVELLERS CHEQUES, ATMS & CREDIT CARDS
Amex and Thomas Cook travellers cheques are accepted in banks, hotels and some exchanges. **Thomas Cook Al-Rostamani** (☎ 222 3564) has numerous branches around the city.

There are globally linked ATMs all over Dubai, at banks, shopping centres and hotels. Visa, MasterCard and Amex are widely accepted and debit cards are accepted at bigger retail outlets.

Newspapers & Magazines
There are several English-language daily newspapers available in Dubai. The best

is the recently launched *Emirates Today*, but most local papers feel more Mumbai than Dubai; newsagents also stock some international newspapers. Locally produced glossies include *Emirates Woman* and *Viva*, and you can check out Dubai's 'celebrities' in *Ahlan!* entertainment magazine. The monthly *Time Out Dubai* has decent listings on upcoming events, as does *What's On*.

Photography & Video

Dubai is a technology-crazed city, so there are memory cards and other accessories for digital cameras on just about every corner. See p39, for specific shops. For the traditionalists, print and slide film as well as processing are widely available. The UAE uses the PAL video system and all imaginable accessories are available. Again, see p39.

Post

Emirates Post is Dubai's often delivery-challenged postal service. There are post boxes at most of the major shopping centres, and stamps are available at card shops as well as post offices. Postcard rates are Dh2 to Europe, the USA, Australia and Asia; Dh1 to Arab countries; and 75 fils within the Gulf. Here are the most useful post offices in Dubai:

Central Post Office (2, B5; Za'abeel Rd, Karama; ✆ 8am-11.30pm Sat-Wed, 8am-10pm Thu, 8am-noon Fri)
Deira Post Office (2, D2; Al-Sabkha Rd, near Baniyas Rd; ✆ 8am-midnight Sat-Wed, 8am-1pm & 4-8pm Thu)

Radio

Dubai's English-language radio stations are bland, with banal programming and 'personalities' that have none – it's more fun to station surf and hear Hindi, Arabic and Indian regional music. The main English-language radio stations are:

Channel 4 FM 104.8
Dubai Eye FM 103.8
Dubai FM 92
Emirates 1 FM 100.5 & 104.1
Emirates 2 FM 90.5 & 98.5

Smoking

Dubai Municipality announced its decision to ban smoking in all leisure and entertainment areas in Dubai from October 2004. By the end of 2004, however, it was clear that the municipality was disinclined to enforce the ban. Shopping malls and restaurants have generally embraced the notion of smoke-free areas, but the onus is on the venues to handle the smoking issue any way they wish. Smoking *sheesha* is a popular local pastime that is often offered in the courtyards or pavements of cafés. While its sweet aromas may be pleasant, some say smoking *sheesha* can be more harmful than cigarettes.

Telephone

The UAE's telecommunications system is run by the state telecommunications company, **Etisalat** (2, D4; cnr Baniyas & Omar ibn al-Khattab Rds; ✆ 24hr). Local calls from residences in Dubai are free (excluding mobile calls). Public phones are mostly card phones, and phonecards (Dh30 and Dh60) are sold at grocery shops and supermarkets – don't buy them from street vendors.

MOBILE PHONES

Mobile phones are the de facto standard in Dubai – when giving someone your number it's assumed that it's for a mobile not a fixed line. Dubai's mobile system is GSM, and roaming agreements exist with many other countries. Mobile numbers begin with 050 in the UAE.

You can buy a prepaid SIM card from Etisalat, called Wasel GSM. The service costs Dh185 and includes the SIM card and Dh10 credit. Recharge cards are available in denominations of Dh30 and Dh60 from grocery stores and supermarkets.

The UAE's WAP service is available to Wasel GSM users as well as normal UAE-based GSM subscribers. Dial ☎ 125 and follow the instructions.

COUNTRY & CITY CODES
To dial another country from the UAE direct, dial ☎ 00, followed by the country code. If you want to call the UAE, the country code is ☎ 971. The area code for Dubai is ☎ 04, but if you're calling from outside the UAE you drop the zero.

USEFUL PHONE NUMBERS
Directory inquiries ☎ 181
International operator ☎ 100

Television
Hotels in Dubai have satellite TV showing news, sitcoms and movies. The most popular packages are from Showtime, Star and Orbit.

Time
Dubai is four hours ahead of GMT and there is no daylight saving.

Tipping
In restaurants tips are not generally expected as a service charge is added to your bill (however, this goes to the restaurant, not the waiter). If you want to leave a tip, 10% is ample for good service. Taxi drivers will make a vague attempt to give you change, but have already mentally rounded up your fare to the nearest Dh5. Valets, hotel porters and the like will expect and appreciate a tip of Dh2 and upwards.

Toilets
The few public toilets on the streets are usually only for men, but public toilets in shopping centres, museums, restaurants and hotels are Western style and are generally well maintained.

Tourist Information
The official tourism board of the Dubai government is the **Department of Tourism & Commerce Marketing** (DTCM; ☎ 223 0000; www.dubaitourism.ae). As well as the main welcome bureaus listed below, most of Dubai's malls have tourism desks with maps and information.
Airport (2, F6; ☎ 224 5252/224 4098; Dubai International Airport; ☾ 24hr)
Baniyas Square (2, D2; ☎ 228 5000; Baniyas Sq; ☾ 9am-11pm)

Women Travellers
In general Dubai is a great destination for women travellers. However, Dubai is a Muslim state and while you will see women dressed in skimpy clothes everywhere, most Emiratis *do* find it offensive (see p26). While you might get a few stares (especially if you don't follow the dress code), physical harassment of women is rare in Dubai.

Feminine hygiene products are freely available throughout Dubai and many forms of contraceptive pill are sold over the counter in pharmacies. For a Muslim city, a startling array of condoms is available in most supermarkets and pharmacies.

LANGUAGE
Arabic is the official language, but English is the language you'll generally hear the most of – as well as a bit of Hindi and Urdu. Signs are nearly always in both Arabic and English. While it's great to learn some easy phrases in Arabic (and much appreciated by Emiratis), it's worth remembering that most people you'll deal with might not speak the language.

Basics
Hello/Welcome.	*marHaba*
Goodbye.	*fl'man ullah* or
	ma'al salaama
Goodbye. (response)	
(to a man)	*alla ysalmak*
(to a woman)	*alla ysalmich*
Please.	
(to a man)	*min fadhlak*
(to a woman)	*min fadhlich*

Thank you (very much).	*shukran (jazeelan)*
You're welcome.	*afwan*
Excuse me.	
(to a man)	*lau tismaH*
(to a woman)	*lau tismaHin*
Yes.	*na'am*
No.	*la'*
Do you speak English?	*titkallam ingleezi?*
Do you understand?	*Hal bitifhaam?*
I understand.	
(by a man)	*ana fahim*
(by a woman)	*ana fahma*
I don't understand.	
(by a man)	*ana mu fahim*
(by a woman)	*ana mu fahma*

Could you please ...?
mumkin min fadhlak ...?

repeat that	*a'id Hatha*
speak more slowly	*takalam shwai shwai*
write it down	*iktbHa lee*

Question Words

Who?	*mnu?*
What?	*shnu?*
When?	*mata?*
Where?	*wayn?*
How?	*chayf?*
How many?	*cham?*

Going Out

What's on ...?
maza yaHdos ...?

locally	*mahaleeyan*
this weekend	*fee nihayet Hatha alesboo'a*
today	*al-yom*
tonight	*al-layla*
Where are the places to eat?	*wayn el maHalat al-aakl?*

Getting Around

Are you free? (taxi)	*anta fathee?*
Please put the meter on.	*lau samaHt shagal al-addad*
How much is it to ...?	*bcham la ...?*
Please take me to (this address).	*lau samaHt wasalni la (Hadha elonwan)*

Numbers

0	٠	*sifr*
1	١	*waHid*
2	٢	*ithneen*
3	٣	*thalatha*
4	٤	*arba'a*
5	٥	*khamsa*
6	٦	*sitta*
7	٧	*sab'a*
8	٨	*thimania*
9	٩	*tis'a*
10	١٠	*ashra*
100	١٠٠	*imia*
1000	١٠٠٠	*alf*

Days

Monday	*yom al-ithneen*
Tuesday	*yom al-thalath*
Wednesday	*yom al-arbaa'*
Thursday	*yom al-khamis*
Friday	*yom al-jama'a*
Saturday	*yom as-sabt*
Sunday	*yom al-Had*

Banking

I want to ...
ana areed an ...

change money	*asref beezat*
change some travellers cheques	*asref chekat siyaHeeya*

Communications

I want to buy a (phone card).
ana areed ashtaree (beetaget Hatef/kart telefon)
I want to make a call (to ...)
ana areed an atsell (bee ...)
I want to make a reverse-charge/collect call.
ana areed taHweel kulfet al-mukalama ila al-mutagee
Where's the local Internet café?
wayn magHa al-internet?

Where can I find a/an ...?
wayn mumkin an ajed ...?
I'd like a/an ...
ana areed ...
   adaptor plug
   aakhaz tawseel
   charger for my phone
   shaHen leel Hatef
   mobile/cell phone for hire
   mobail ('mobile') leel ajar
   prepaid mobile/cell phone
   mobail moos baq aldaf'
   SIM card for your network
   seem kart lee shabaket al-itsalaat

Food

breakfast	*futtoor*
lunch	*ghadha*
dinner	*asha*

Emergencies

It's an emergency!
Halet isa'af!
Call the (police/a doctor/an ambulance)!
etasell bil (shurta/tabeeb/sayyaret al-isa'af)!

Health

Where's the nearest ...?
wayn aghrab ...?

chemist (night)	*saydalee (laylee)*
doctor	*tabeeb*
hospital	*mustashfa*

I have (a) ...
ana andee ...

diarrhoea	*is-haal*
fever	*sukhoona*
headache	*suda or waja' ras*
pain	*alam/waja'*

Index

See also separate indexes for Eating (p92), Entertainment (p92), Shopping (p92), Sights with map references (p93) and Sleeping (p93).

EATING

ENTERTAINMENT

SHOPPING

SIGHTS

SLEEPING

FEATURES

- Lime Tree Café .... *Eating*
- iBo .... *Entertainment*
- Ku Bu .... *Drinking*
- Kanzaman .... *Café*
- Dubai Museum .... *Highlights*
- Bur Dubai Souq .... *Shopping*
- Majlis Gallery .... *Sights/Activities*
- Grand Hyatt Dubai .... *Sleeping*

AREAS

.... Beach, Desert
.... Building
.... Land
.... Mall
.... Other Area
.... Park/Cemetery
.... Sports
.... Urban

HYDROGRAPHY

.... River, Creek
.... Intermittent River
.... Canal
.... Swamp
.... Water

BOUNDARIES

.... State, Provincial
.... Regional, Suburb
.... Ancient Wall

ROUTES

.... Tollway
.... Freeway
.... Primary Road
.... Secondary Road
.... Tertiary Road
.... Lane
.... Under Construction
.... One-Way Street
.... Unsealed Road
.... Mall/Steps
.... Tunnel
.... Walking Path
.... Walking Trail/Track
.... Pedestrian Overpass
.... Walking Tour

TRANSPORT

.... Airport, Airfield
.... Bus Route
.... Cycling, Bicycle Path
.... Ferry
.... General Transport
.... Metro
.... Monorail
.... Rail
.... Taxi Rank
.... Tram

SYMBOLS

- .... Bank, ATM
- .... Beach
- .... Buddhist
- .... Castle, Fortress
- .... Christian
- .... Diving, Snorkelling
- .... Embassy, Consulate
- .... Hindu
- .... Hospital, Clinic
- .... Information
- .... Internet Access
- .... Islamic
- .... Monument
- .... Mountain, Volcano
- .... National Park
- .... Parking Area
- .... Petrol Station
- .... Picnic Area
- .... Point of Interest
- .... Police Station
- .... Post Office
- .... Ruin
- .... Sikh
- .... Telephone
- .... Toilets
- .... Zoo, Bird Sanctuary
- .... Waterfall

24/7 travel advice
www.lonelyplanet.com